San Juan Antigua
Old San Juan, Puerto Rico
2011 EDITION + BONUS CHAPTER

Paseo de la Princessa Fountain

San Juan Antigua

Old San Juan, Puerto Rico

2011 EDITION + BONUS CHAPTER

Have an Adventure
In a far-off, but not too distant land

James L. Tate

Copyright © 2011 by James L. Tate

All rights reserved. No part of this publication may be reproduced, stored in a retrieval system or transmitted in any form or by any means electronic, mechanical, photocopying, recording or otherwise, without the prior written permission of the copyright holder.

ISBN-10: 0-9818816-3-7
ISBN-13: 978-0-9818816-3-8

Published by
Acacia Multimedia Publishing
PO Box 563
Boca Raton, Florida 33429

Cover and interior design by Acacia Multimedia Publishing

Printed in the United Sates of America

Guardian of the Spanish Main and a Defense of the First Order

This book is dedicated to the twenty-five generations of *Sanjuanearos* who from the days of *Ponce de Leon* have for five-hundred years encountered both tumultuous historic moments and long periods of relative tranquility, and while residing, working, and experiencing all the joy and sorrow that life has to offer contributed one and all to making Old San Juan the special place that it is, and will always be.

La Garita—Sentry Box

Contents

Preface…….. 9

Introduction…….. 11

Chapter One…….. 15
Beyond Expectations
(Más Allá de Expectativas)

Chapter Two…….. 39
Best of all Worlds
(Mejor de todos los Mundos)

Chapter Three…….. 57
(Pasaportes, Visados, y Norteamericanos)

Chapter Four…….. 77
Donkeys, Americans, and Sunburns
(Burros, Gringos, y Quemaduras de Sol)

Chapter Five…….. 91
Dollars, Quarters, and Pennies
(Pesos, Pesetas, y Centavos)

Conclusion…….. 107
Expat Newspapers & Gourmet Coffee
(Periódicos de Expat y Café de Gastrónomo)

About the Author…….. 111
Seagulls and Sunsets
(Gaviotas y Ocasos)

Bonus Chapter…….. 115
Who are the Puerto Ricans?
(¿Quiénes son los puertorriqueños?)

Casa Blanca Gardens

Preface

Beyond all of the emotions and expectations that living as an expatriate in Old San Juan satisfied and fulfilled there was a simple act that I especially treasured. In the early dawn from my bedroom balcony that overlooked the lush tropical gardens of the historic *Casa Blanca*, I would often sip my morning cup of Puerto Rican coffee *(café Puertoriqueno)* while reading the morning edition of the Pulitzer Prize wining expat newspaper, *The San Juan Star*. As the sky brightened, one could also begin to hear the audible stir of life that for five-hundred years accompanied the awakening of this world-renowned Spanish colonial walled city. Now, over three decades later, the same rich experiences that make up some of my fondest and most vivid memories are still at hand in *San Juan Antigua*, this far off, but not to distant land.

James L. Tate
San Juan Antigua
March, 2011

Ponce de Leon—San Jose Plaza

Introduction

Knowing about and appreciating Old San Juan's distinctive endowments, its Spanish colonial architecture, plus its rich and intriguing history adds much to the enjoyment of living there. As a result, this book may take on some of the characteristics of a history lesson. If history and human drama does not interest you, then Old San Juan may not be a good choice as an expatiate location to consider. If, on the other hand, you are somewhat of a history buff and adventure stories of swashbuckling Caribbean privateers and pirates, tales of empire building, colonial powers and conquest, intermixed with Latin love stories and romantic novellas gains your attention than Old San Juan should fit the bill. There is no way to find out about living in *San Juan Antigua,* without learning something about its dramatic past and the historic figures associated to the city, such as Juan Ponce de Leon and Sir Francis Drake. The first two chapters reveal stories of these famous personalities and their influence on the founding and character of the colonial city, and much more.

Old San Juan is not an archeological dig, but a living city; therefore, this book serves another important purpose. It will give those persons searching for an extraordinary expatriate experience enough information about present-day life in the walled city to inspire them to investigate further. The last three chapters provide up to date facts and insights.

Plaza San Jose

The book relates to the reader both the historical attraction of this appealing colonial tropical city and the enriched living experience it can offer an expatriate. Coupled with its exclusive past is interwoven a very with-it Latino cultural setting with contemporary artists, musicians, global brand stores and one of a kind boutiques. For those who enjoy gourmet eating Old San Juan has a host of restaurants offering twenty-first century culinary fare. All of this and more are intermixed within a physically charming environment that as a city is very manageable if not almost, because of its architectural scale, compassionate to human life.

Moving to almost any place that is unfamiliar to us both challenges our sensibilities and stimulates our senses. The differences in the style of the local architecture, new colors, novel sounds, or even very ordinary and mundane things like parking requirements can all seem often unsettling. In Puerto Rico, as an example, it is legal to park on either side of the street facing each way. In Manhattan, where I moved from, if you park you car facing the opposite way from the flow of traffic you could expect to get a ticket. Many *Sanjuaneuros* who moved to New York City did and still do. When added to the list of other variants that—in an exciting way—can visually assault you, something as simple as this I found initially disorienting upon first arriving on the island thirty-four years ago. Later I began to welcome this state of mind where things seemed initially confusing, because I knew it was a sign of personal intellectual growth and spiritual development.

Police cars in Puerto Rico have blue flashing lights, not the red ones that I was accustomed to back in New York. They drive around with the lights on all the time, not just when they are answering a call or in pursuit, and the sound of their sirens are more similar in tone to those that you hear in Europe.

On the island, there is a unique species of tree frogs known as the Coqui. Less than an inch long, it is very popular throughout Puerto Rico because it serenades islanders to sleep. The name "Coqui" comes from the love song that the male of the species sings, from sunset to sunrise. It seems to say is "Ko-kee, Ko-kee." This is how you pronounce *Coqui* in Spanish. Although some Coquies have been successfully exported to other countries, legend has it that they can never sing once removed from the Island.

Hosts of sensory impressions, some of which like the graceful melody of the Coqui were relatively subtle, yet they all contributed to the extraordinary ambience and wonderland sensation that engulfed me during the years that I contentedly resided and worked in Old San Juan. These seemingly minor tangible differences, ranging from parking requirements to blue flashing lights of police cars, initiated the beginning of my journey as an expat. What began like the outgoing tide slowly swept me away from the safe harbor of my earlier mono-cultural existence. I found myself out into the vast and sometimes turbulent sea of a multi-cultural life of unfamiliar sights and strange sounds. Most challenging to me was deciphering and codifying the different points of view on almost everything that were coming at me from this new and rich culture that I was attempting to embrace after moving to *San Juan Antigua*.

San Cristobal Fortress

Chapter 1

Beyond Expectations
(Más Allá de Expectativas)

Steeped in history with an old world ambiance and romantic European charm this "Guardian of the Spanish Main," is one of only two walled cities *(ciudades amuralladas)* in the western hemisphere, with the other being Cartagena, Columbia. Encompassing a square mile, Old San Juan is the larger. Chartered by the Spanish Crown, the conquistadors built these cities as siege fortifications or as described in Spanish military lingo a "Defense of the First Order." With five other primary forts plus fourteen secondary forts that the Spaniards built throughout the Caribbean, along the coasts of South and Central America, and extending as far north as St. Augustine, Florida, their strategic purpose was to protect Spain's emerging interests in what for Europeans was the New World. For almost four hundred years, they successfully fulfilled their mission.

With no two buildings being exactly alike, Old San Juan is an architectural treasure with over four-hundred sixteenth and seventeenth century Spanish colonial structures, two world-renowned fortifications, four main plazas, fountains reminiscent of Rome, and blue cobble-stoned streets in addition to ocean vistas and bay views. Protected within the walls that in the past nobly defended this city, is a universally recognized unique urban habitat with more history and culture than an expat can absorb in a lifetime. With the exception of maybe Tangiers, there is no other place on earth quite like it. In 1521, another expatriate Juan Ponce de Leon founded the city, which eventually would become the most coveted of all of Spain's colonial outposts, and whereas he may not have discovered the fountain of youth on his later expeditions to Florida, in many ways this intrepid explorer's influence is still very much alive in *San Juan Antigua*.

My personal connection to this best known of all conquistadors is that I lived in a four hundred year old restored colonial townhouse that was four doors away from the gated entrance to the Ponce de León family estate, which has now existed for almost five centuries. The land was a grant to Ponce de León as a reward for services rendered to the Spanish Crown. For almost two hundred fifty years, his direct descendents lived there making it the longest occupied private residence in the western hemisphere. Between then and until very recently, first the Spanish in 1779, and then in 1898, because of the Spanish American War the American military occupied the mini-fort-like compound that itself was Puerto Rico's first defensive structure. Its design accommodated the storage of military weapons and government funds in addition to being a home. Today, the Institute of Puerto Rican Culture maintains the colonial buildings and exotic tropical gardens that make up this unique inner city property as a museum known as the *Casa Blanca*. A few blocks away in the San Juan Cathedral, whose construction began circa 1520, rests Juan Ponce de Leon's interned remains.

Larger-Than-Life Location
(Posición Grande Que Vida)

One could hardly find a larger-than-life location *(posición grande que vida)* and wonderful cultural setting for an expatriate experience. Residing in Old San Juan is like playing a role in an epic motion picture, and living there is similar to being on a Hollywood movie set. Resembling in shape a peninsula, this extraordinary city is on the westerly tip of what is actually a small island. It connects to the mainland of Puerto Rico by a short causeway that spans over the mouth of the scenic San Juan Lagoon, which is almost a mile long by a half a mile wide. Circling the lagoon is an esplanade that is especially delightful at night, as it is a favorite place for lovers to walk hand in hand. During the day, people enjoy all types of activities from water skiing to running about in Jet Ski type watercrafts, which various establishments that are adjacent to the lagoon will rent.

Old San Juan

Approximately one hundred miles long and thirty-five miles wide, Puerto Rico is the smallest and most eastern island of the Greater Antilles, which includes Cuba and Hispaniola—the island that Haiti and the Dominican Republic share. The island is the western edge of the Lesser Antilles. This chain of islands or archipelago begins with the United States and British Virgin Islands directly east of Puerto Rico and extends in a

Beyond Expectations

sweeping 800 miles long arch to the islands of Trinidad and Tobago, which are off the coast of Venezuela, and then continue east to Aruba. Puerto Rico is almost dead center in the area known as the Caribbean, which got its name from the Caribs, one of the dominant Amerindian groups in the region at the time of European contact during the late fifteenth Century. The Carib Indians played a role in the early colonial development of Old San Juan, which will be more fully explained in a following chapter. The analogous "West Indies" originates from Christopher Columbus' notion that he had actually landed in the Indies (then meaning all of south and east Asia) when he had actually reached the Americas.

After the Columbus expedition, the European powers realized that the dispersed lands comprised an extensive archipelago enclosing the Caribbean Sea and the Gulf of Mexico. Thereafter, the term *Antilles* was commonly assigned to the formation, and "Sea of the Antilles" became a common alternate name for the Caribbean Sea in various European languages.

The word *Antilles* originated in the period before the European conquest of the New World—Antilia being one of those mysterious lands which figured on the medieval charts, sometimes as an archipelago, sometimes as continuous land of greater or lesser extent, its location fluctuating in mid-ocean between the Canary Islands and India.

The Caribbean (Dutch : *Cariben* or *Caraïben*, or more commonly *Antillen*; French: *Caraibe* or more commonly *Antilles*; Spanish: *Caribe*) is a region of the Americas consisting of the Caribbean Sea, its Dutch, French, English, and Spanish islands (most of which enclose the sea), and the surrounding coasts. The region is located southeast of North America, east of Central America, and to the north and west of South America.

Situated largely on the Caribbean Plate, and incorporating more than 7,000 islands, islets, reefs, and cays, the West Indies encompasses an area of approximately one third the size of the United States. In addition to the Greater Antilles, which bound the Caribbean sea on the north and the Lesser Antilles on the south and east, both the Bahamas and Bermuda each of which lie much further to the north in the Atlantic are considered in the West Indies. Some people also view the small chain of islands at the foot of Florida, which end in Key West as being Caribbean.

Geopolitically, the West Indies are usually reckoned as a sub region of North America and are organized into 28 territories including sovereign states, overseas departments, and dependencies. At one time, there was a short-lived country called the Federation of the West Indies composed of ten English-speaking Caribbean territories.

In the English-speaking Caribbean, someone from the area is usually referred to as a "West Indian", although the rather cumbersome phrase "Caribbean person" is sometimes used. The use of the words "Caribbean" and "Caribbean's" to refer to a West Indian or West Indians is largely known in the English-speaking Caribbean. On more than one occasion I was corrected, however, when I referred to persons from the Bahamas, as being West Indian.

Some Spanish-speaking Caribbean residents do not like to be called Hispanics or Latinos due to the significant differences with South and Central American countries. Spanish-speaking Caribbean people differ significantly from mainland Latin Americans in many aspects of ethnicity, history, dialects of Spanish spoken, culture, and traditions. Among Caribbean Spanish speaking persons from the three island countries of Cuba, the Dominican Republic, and Puerto Rico, there are also cultural differences, most of which in my opinion are fostered more by intense feelings of nationalistic pride, rather than by cultural realities.

Puerto Rico and Old San Juan's location—being in the center of the Caribbean—played an important role in the development of the New World, and likewise their proximity to the rest of the Caribbean offers a unique feature for an expatriate experience, which a following chapter will fully explore. San Juan also has the dubious reputation of being the bottom point of the Bermuda Triangle, sometimes referred to as the Devil's Triangle. The other two points are Miami and Bermuda. Christopher Columbus himself was the first person to document something strange in the Triangle, reporting that he and his crew observed "strange dancing lights on the horizon", flames in the sky, and at another point he wrote in his log about bizarre compass bearings in the area.

In addition to all of this, Old San Juan's geography itself gives it an uncanny and perfect configuration to be a walled city. It is as if nature, if not destiny, intended it. At its elevated northwest point, and some one hundred feet above sea level, sits the world famous fort and castle known as *Castillo de San Felipe del Morro*.

El Morro Fortress

El Morro, the word itself sounds powerful, and the six-level fortress that commands the imposing high ground at the entrance to San Juan Bay certainly is. With an impressive battery of cannon positions, its construction began in 1539 and spanned a period of two historic centuries of empire and conquest. Its sole purpose was to protect both the bay and the city itself from enemy attack. Felipe II (1527—98) was the king of Spain during its "Golden Age," and in addition to the Philippines; *Castillo de Felipe del Morro* bore his name. Before Felipe, no other monarch had ever dealt with so widespread an empire that encircled almost all the way around the globe. His contemporaries included Shakespeare and Queen Elizabeth I, whose refusal of his marriage offer lead to an act of retribution that went badly for the king with the defeat of the Spanish Armada.

Sir Francis Drake played a key role as Vice Admiral of the British fleet during the battle that contributed to the 1588 routing of Spain's royal navy, and although the Spanish monarch considered him only a pirate, Drake was the king's life long nemesis. All hope that Felipe may have had to take Elizabeth by force if not by seduction Drake dashed, but the Spanish monarch would have a smaller but sweet revenge, and the fort named in his honor at the mouth of the San Juan Bay would play a decisive role. Old San Juan is awash with five centuries of history that began with the age of exploration, upon which the foundation for our era is resting, and when you reside there, you find yourself unexpectedly immersed in its dramatic and theatrical-like past.

Although I had lived in Manhattan's Greenwich Village before coming to San Juan, there was a distinct psychological difference in residing inside a walled city rather than only living in an enclave of a big city. Cities—of almost any size—have within them distinct neighborhoods, which are not necessarily ethnic, but still posses their very own makeup and distinct character. A unique feeling that was womb-like in nature came over me whenever I would return to the Old San Juan, even if I were away for only a few hours. It was a similar but much more intense sensation than that which I felt upon emerging from the subway station at Christopher Street and Sheridan Square in the West Village on my way home from my midtown job.

The City Walls

Today, the West Village, as well as the East Village, has experienced a gentrification, with the bohemians, artists, beatniks, and hippies being long gone. The original coffee houses that earlier had displayed abstract expressionist paintings of the 1950s rebel artists such as Jackson Pollard, in which beat poets like Allen Ginsberg read their mostly angst ridden poems, and later folk singers the likes of Bob Dylan for a free meal performed while playing his acoustic guitar are now Starbucks frequented by investment bankers.

San Juan City Hall

Old San Juan still has the artists, writers, and especially Latino jazz musicians, along with a substantial working class population with street vendors selling *piraguas* from their colorful carts. These hand shaved ice snow cones come with a wide assortment of very sweet tropical fruit syrup flavorings. My favorite topping was mango with pineapple being a close runner up. On many a warm tropical afternoon I would often enjoy the cool refreshing treat while relaxing on a tree shaded bench in the *Plaza de Armas* across from San Juan's mayor's office, which was a short stroll from my design studio. Construction of the municipal  building began in 1602 and ended in 1789. Its present day façade, remodeled in the 1840s, is an exact replica of Madrid's city hall.

Alluring and Sultry Ambiance
(La Fascinación y Ambiente Bochornoso)

The weather is another important factor that contributes to both the Caribbean's allure *(la fascinación)* and Old San Juan's sultry ambiance *(ambience bochornoso.)* Puerto Rico's has a tropical marine climate with an average temperature of 80°F (26°C). The island enjoys warm and sunny days throughout most of the year, and although lightweight clothing is appropriate year-round, Puerto Ricans, men and women alike, are very fashion conscious and dress accordingly well. They take great personal care in how they look. Suits and ties are standard apparel in business and patterned dress shirts and creased slacks are common public male attire. Women in San Juan are very stylish and dress for work similar to those in Manhattan, Paris, or Buenos Aires. There is a very active fashion industry in Puerto Rico, with world class designers whose fashions appear everywhere. It is a sense of both pride and respect for others that drives this fashion consciousness, which even includes construction workers. Working class people also dress up going to their job, and once there they change into their work clothes. After work, they change back into their more formal street wear for the commute home.

Beyond the shore, in the interior of Puerto Rico, the idyllic temperature is between 73°F and 78°F (22°C and 25°C). Inland or on the coast, the relative humidity is high, about 80% throughout the year. The ever-blowing trade winds that for most of the year originate from the east moderate the temperature, and to feel comfortable outside you only need to step into the shade.

When people visiting the island would ask me when the rainy season was, I would tell them that it ran from January thru December. It rains throughout the year, but normally doubles from May to October, which coincides with hurricane season. January Thru April is the comparatively driest period, which concludes with the arrival of the Easter winds that originate out of the southwest. The *Sierra de Luquillo* mountain range along Puerto Rico's northern coast, where the world famous rain forest *El Yunque* is, gets twice as much rain as the south coast, which has a distinct arid landscape. Even on islands in the Caribbean that are considerably smaller than Puerto Rico, like St. Johns, which is forty miles east and the smallest of the United States' Virgin Islands, you will find lush vegetation on the windward side of the island were it normally rains. Six miles across the island on its leeward side, it is desert like with cactus growing. Annual precipitation on the north coast of Puerto Rico, where Old San Juan is located is sixty-one inches, in the south thirty-six, and in the mountains as much as two hundred inches.

Luquillo Rain Forest

During the twenty-five years that I lived in Puerto Rico, there were droughts that required the rationing of water, and excessive rainy periods that caused flooding, landslides, and deaths. Because of its elevation above sea level, Old San Juan never floods, and there is usually a wonderful breeze. Tropical showers that may last from a few minutes to a half hour are common, but seldom does it rain non-stop all day, except during infrequent large tropical storms. People hardly ever wear raincoats, yet you may want to own an umbrella. Fog is common in the inland valleys of Puerto Rico, but it normally dissipates by early morning as the sun rises over the mountains. Although US Coast Guard regulations require that all Puerto Rican pleasure boats have bells, you never have fog offshore, disregarding what you may have seen in Caribbean pirate movies.

Each year around June, Sahara dust storms that originate in northeast Africa sweep across Morocco and the Canary Islands before crossing the Atlantic Ocean, and often for as long as two weeks the sky over Puerto Rico and much of the Caribbean can have a distinct sand-like color haze. The dust clouds follow the same atmospheric path as the Atlantic hurricanes that also begin their lives off the coast of northeast Africa, which is some two thousand miles directly east of Puerto Rico.

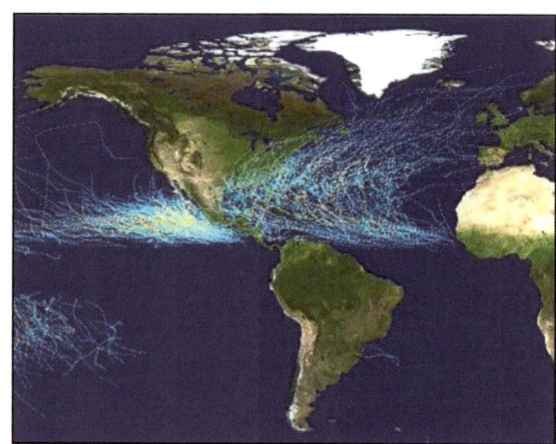

The frequency of hurricanes in Puerto Rico is less than Jamaica, Cuba, and the Lesser Antilles. The storms generally occur between August and October, although the United States' National Weather Service considers the hurricane season for the North Atlantic Basin, which includes the Atlantic Ocean, the Caribbean Sea, and the Gulf of Mexico, to run from June 1 to November 30. Hurricane seasons over the past decade have averaged 13.6 tropical storms with 35–65 mph winds, 7.8 hurricanes with winds greater than 65 mph, and 3.8 major hurricanes with winds exceeding 100 mph.

Since the keeping of weather related records, dozens of hurricanes struck the island, but probably the most destructive was *San Ciriaco*, which came ashore on August 8, 1899. The cyclone kept tropical storm strength or higher for twenty-eight days of almost constant rain, which makes it the longest duration on record for Puerto Rico and the second-longest anywhere in the world. During the height of the storm, the winds reached speeds of one hundred miles an hour. The loss of life and property damage was extensive with thirty-four hundred people dying, and many more left homeless, without food and work. The storm destroyed the sugar and coffee crops, which at that time the island and its people depended upon.

When hurricanes or even tropical storms do occur, Old San Juan is one of the safest places to live. In addition to being one hundred feet above sea level, rendering the city not subject to storm surges, the massive masonry construction of the homes and buildings make them almost indestructible to hurricane force winds. In addition most buildings have sturdy wood planked doors and wood louver windows that shut tight. During very heavy downpours, interior courtyards, although depressed and drained, may still accumulate some water, but all adjacent floors are either marble or some type of ceramic or quarry tile, and being so are not subject to water damage. Forty reported hurricanes have hit the island since the Spaniards began keeping records. Some like *San Ciriaco* left many dead with most of the casualties along the coast.

The island has also suffered a number of minor temblors that crack walls and send hanging plants to sway; something that I have disconcertingly witnessed more than once. Old San Juan faces very little urban seismic risk, because of the heavy masonry construction with some of the main supporting bearing walls of the colonial buildings being over eighteen inches thick. Couple this with the fact that buildings are built up against each other, and the mass that this creates is such that it would take a severe earthquake in the range of eight or greater on the Richter Scale to cause any serious damage. Puerto Rico is located on the edge of the Caribbean Plate, which is moving to the northeast. Apparently, because there are enough small movements between the Caribbean and the adjacent Atlantic Plate they prevent any large slipping in the fault plane that can result in catastrophic damage. In 1867, an earthquake whose epicenter was located in the Anegada Passage between Puerto Rico and St. Croix in the Virgin Islands caused a tsunami that came ashore on the south coast. Although it swept five hundred feet inland, there was little personal property damage with no loss of life recorded. A series of earthquakes shook the western part of the island again in 1918 during the course of a week, but this time there was considerable damage and some loss of life when another tidal wave swept into the west coast.

Every year in many Third World countries, there are disaster stories about the destruction of whole villages with reports of thousands of casualties. Always the earthquake catches the blame for the death and destruction. It is not the temblor, however, that killed the people, but the houses and buildings that fell done on top of them. Often these structures made from an adobe type of sun dried mud brick or rubble masonry likewise have no reinforcing steel. Wood beams being held in place with only mortar while sitting on top of the unstable walls support second floors and roofs. When the shaking starts, the walls begin to crumble and the upper floors and roof pancake down to the ground. In addition to the unnecessary lost of life, the sad ending of the distressing chronicle is that after the earthquake the same house is rebuilt in the same way with the same bricks and beams that fell down. Ten or twenty years later, it happens again, and for thousands of years the same cycle repeats itself. India, Pakistan, and Iran are three of the countries where these disasters regularly occur, and although they have nuclear weapons or are developing them, they cannot build safe housing. This includes China where in May of 2008 at least fifty-thousand people lost there lives when many state built buildings including schools simply collapsed killing or trapping those inside.

Antigua Guatemala, in Guatemala, is also a Spanish Colonial city with structures similar to Old San Juan. Throughout its history large earthquakes repeatedly damaged the city and although the *Antigueños* rebuilt, on July 29, 1773 an earthquake wrought such destruction that officials petitioned the King of Spain to allow them to move the capital to safer ground, which led to the founding in 1776 of present-day Guatemala City. Most citizens left, but they did not completely abandon Antigua. Today its monumental bougainvillea-draped ruins, and its preserved and carefully restored Spanish colonial public buildings and private mansions give form to a city of charm and romance similar to *San Juan Antigua*, but on a much smaller scale. Old San Juan buildings rest on a rock promontory, which is why it is more resistant to earthquake forces, whereas *Antigua Guatemala* is located, not only in a valley, but also directly below three volcanic mountains. Of the three, the *Volcan de Fuego* or "Volcano of Fire," is some 12,346 feet high. *"Fuego"* as it is called locally, is famous for being almost constantly active at a low level. Smoke issues from its top daily, but larger eruptions are rare. There are no active or dormant volcanoes anywhere near Old San Juan.

Volcano of Fire—Antigua Guatemala

On December 23, 1972, a series of devastating earthquakes that lasted for twenty days shook Managua, Nicaragua, with approximately 5,000 fatalities. After the earthquakes, an assessment made indicated that the older colonial buildings held up better that some of the newer structures. Puerto Rico has a connection to the Managua earthquake. Roberto Clemente the famous Puerto Rican major league baseball player lost his life when a chartered plane he was in that was bringing relief supplies to Managua crashed on takeoff from the San Juan International Airport.

There is consideration given to earthquakes in the design of buildings in Puerto Rico, which has an up to date comprehensive building code, but the main concern for the island's architects and engineers is to design buildings to resist hurricane wind loading. The structural engineers are not as troubled with buildings settling because of bad soils, as much as they are with the building flying away. The uplift forces caused by hurricane wind loading are often greater than the weight of the building on the subsoil.

Outside of the hurricanes, which are less frequent than in other parts of the Caribbean, the weather in Puerto Rico is just wonderful, and it is so predictable that, you never even think about it. There is no need to have separate winter and summer wardrobes, since throughout the year the weather hardly changes. Old San Juan and its climate is a perfect match, both are alluring and sultry.

Buccaneer's Prize
(Premio de un Bucanero)

Part of being successful in living in a far off and distant land comes from gaining an understanding of ones new surroundings and the idiosyncrasy of an unfamiliar culture. A dual experience not every person who leaves home for a foreign country has. The all-encompassing physical environment of Old San Juan is both intense and inclusive, and grasping how important the old city is to Puerto Ricans is a first step in coming to not only know them, but also something new about yourself as well. The world-renowned *El Morro* fort has a feature called a *"garita,"* which are small circular sentry boxes that are strategically located around the walls of the fort. It has become an important national symbol. Many see it as not only being what its original intended use was, a lookout from which the posted colonial guards would scan the ocean watching for first warning signs of an invasion fleet's top sails breaking the distant horizon, but today its symbolism is as  a sentinel that guards the Puerto Rican culture. All Puerto Ricans hold in pride this remarkable fort, which encompasses seventy-four acres. In 1949 it was designated a National Historic Site by the Unites States government with the unique distinction of being the largest fortification in the Caribbean. Later, in 1992, and in honor of the five hundredth anniversary of the discovery of Puerto Rico by Christopher Columbus, a restoration of the fortress to its historical form was completed. This remarkable citadel contributes to the sense of high adventure that living as an expatriate in Old San Juan offers.

Initially, it was the threat from French and English pirates that forced the Spanish Crown to fortify the city, and by the time Sir Francis Drake, the hero of the battle of the Spanish Armada, made his fierce attack of the city in 1595 it had thirty-two cannon. Drake and his cousin Sir John Hawkins, who designed the faster English ships that defeated the Armada in the English Channel, also joined him in many privateer ventures. Moreover, Hawkins has the infamous reputation of being the first major English slave trader. Their fierce and determined attack on Old San Juan was not to subjugate the city, but there was a very specific objective befitting of a privateer or pirate.

The buccaneer's prize *(premio de un bucanero)* was a Spanish galleon that after suffering damage at sea put into Old San Juan with a treasure of two million ducats in gold and silver *(oro y plata)*, which today would be equal to one hundred and fifty million U.S. dollars. Literally it was a fortune, but not all together an unheard of amount during the Spanish occupation of the New World. Commandeering a contingent that was in proportion to the take, Drake launched a land and sea attack with twenty-two vessels and the siege raged on for several days. During a night assault and while under the cover of darkness, Drake was attempting to slip unnoticed into the San Juan Bay, when the Spanish artillerists of the El Morro battery found their range and shot a cannon ball directly through the captain's cabin of Drake's flagship. This narrow escape shook Drake, and as a result, he came to see the futility of his efforts, gave the reluctant order for his fleet to disengage from the battle, and sailed away empty handed — but still breathing — to the west.

When the news reached Madrid of the circumstances of Drake's defeat by the fort named in honor of the Spanish king, it was reported to have given Felipe II some pleasure at a time when very little else within the empire was going well. Belief had it that the joint defeat of the Armada years earlier coupled with the loss of Queen Elizabeth's affections doubly affected Felipe's resilience, and this combination of woes was the match that lit the fuse leading to the eventual implosion

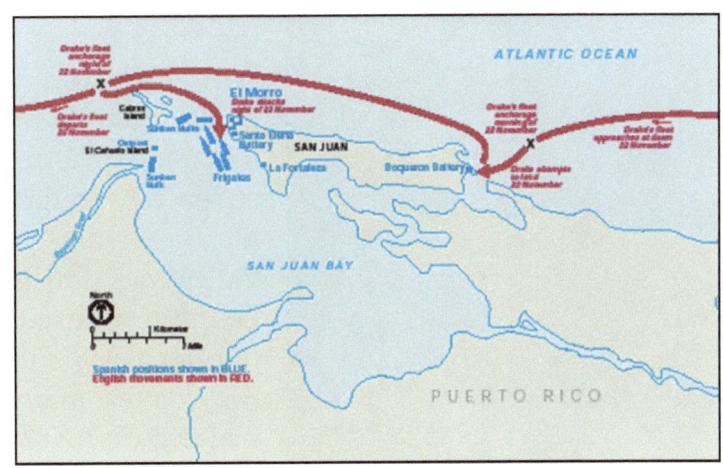

Sir Francis Drake's Attack 1595

Beyond Expectations

of Spain's vast empire, which he ruled. It was in recognizable decline before the king died three years after Drake's roust by the cannons of *Castillo de Felipe del Morro* in Old San Juan. Although the event did not change the now clear direction of where the fortunes of the great naval powers were heading, it was a pointed condolence for this king who many view as being one of the most important monarchs under Christendom of all time.

Queen Elizabeth I

No sovereign, however, has been the object of such diverse judgments. While the Spaniards regarded him as their Solomon and called him "the prudent king," to Protestants he was the "demon of the south" and most cruel of tyrants, because he constituted himself the defender of Catholicism throughout the world of which a good part of it he actually reigned over. What might have been this most famous of all Spanish King's last military victory took place under the ominous walls of *El Morro*. During what turned out to be his final voyage, things for Drake were not going any better than they were for the king that he had relentless harassed for more than a quarter of a century.

King Felipe II

Sir Francis Drake

A year after having his cabin blown out from under him and suffering a string of similar defeats in other parts of the West Indies including the loss of his cousin and cohort, Hawkins, who died off the coast of Puerto Rico, Drake himself died of dysentery near Portobello on Panama's northern coast. In a simple lead coffin, his burial at sea was in the same Caribbean waters where his most daring exploits took place, as one of the great British naval heroes. On the other hand, was Drake simply what Felipe II accused him, an accursed buccaneer? Whatever the verdict, contained within the city walls of *San Juan Antigua* are many captivating tales and intriguing stories waiting discovery, and like the treasure ship that Drake was after, there are a host of expat experiences available for the taking for those who are willing to take the risk.

Unforeseen Rewards
(Recompensas Imprevistas)

In 1978, I took delivery of a new sailboat from a captain that I hired to sail it from Miami to San Juan. A week after it arrived I would have an unanticipated insight into the historical reality of this unique walled city when for the first time I came to not only see, but also to feel the power of *El Morro* from the sea. With a crew of two-friends, our itinerary that Saturday was to make a thirty-five mile voyage along the north coast of Puerto Rico from San Juan to *Isleta Marina*, which is a small island with a marina that is half a mile offshore on the eastern tip of Puerto Rico directly west of the US Virgin Islands. When sailing my thirty-foot sloop out of the San Juan harbor, and coming under the foreboding shadow shed by the fort, I had what I can only describe as a dark epiphany.

An unexpected sense of impending dread came over me that the British and eventually American naval officers and common sailors must have also felt as the imposing battlements rising ten stories above them came into view and their ships fell within range of the fort's deadly barrages. I once read a journal kept by an English midshipman who crewed during the eighteenth century. One particular entry left an impression on me. It was his account of the terror felt by all hands on board after seeing muzzle flash from an enemy ship and hearing the distinct thunder clap like boom of the deck gun discharge while waiting to know of ones own survival or impending doom during the brief but eternal moments until the inevitable arrival of the deadly shot. The remembrance of this naval officer's words came to mind that early morning as I sailed out of the harbors

The Power of El Morro from the sea.

mouth beneath the ominous silhouette of the western face of the great fort that was still in a sinister specter like shadow, which the rising sun behind it was casting.

A very real sense of emotional and physical relief surged within me when I gave the order to tack to a northeasterly course. The maneuver took the boat out into the Atlantic, beyond the fort's eclipsing umbrage and into the still low to the horizon, but bright daybreak sunlight. Once clear of the admittedly imagined apprehension that the commanding presence of *El Morro* had strangely imposed upon me and after winching the jib sheet and securing it to the cleat, I lit a cigarette. Even in its retirement, this phantom fortress at the mouth of the San Juan Bay still has a power to intimidate. In my mind, it would have required unimaginable courage to launch a seaside challenge against these fortifications in ships, whether called "man-o'-war" or galleon, which were still only three to four times longer than my sailboat.

Although my goal that morning was simply to sail my boat to its homeport, the unanticipated experience that I had during the daylong voyage's first half hour was more than I could have hoped. Unforeseen rewards such as these validated my choice to have an expatriate life *(una vida de expatriado,)* and choosing to live in this remarkable city. For sailors, however, San Juan is not the place to keep your boat, because there are no places to sail to on Puerto Rico's north coast. The closest marinas for sailors are in Fajardo, which is a town that is a forty-five minute drive east of San Juan on the island's northeast tip. A

Isleta Marina—Fajardo, Puerto Rico

onetime haven for smugglers and pirates, it is where the infamous nineteenth century Puerto Rican pirate Roberto Cofresi Ramirez de Arellano often hid out.

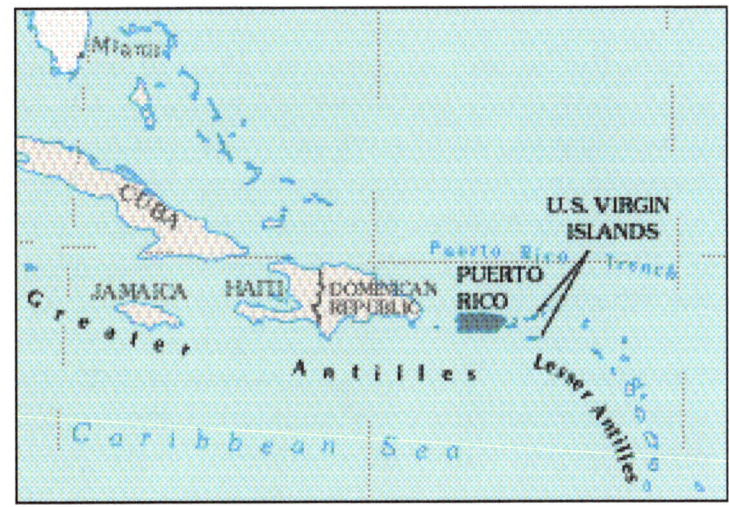

Today, Fajardo still has a strong maritime tradition with many full service marinas and allegedly it is still a port of entry for contraband and illegal aliens. Its proximity to a number of small uninhabited islands, Icacos and Palominos, plus the two Spanish Virgin islands of Culebra and Vieques, and the United States and British Virgin Islands, all within eyesight and the furthest less than a half day's sail away, makes it the most popular location for sailors or yachtsmen from San Juan to keep their boats. People come from all over the world to this part of the Caribbean to charter boats, which from Fajardo east to Tortola and southwest to St. Croix is a sailor's paradise. Within this triangle whose three sides are less than forty miles long there are almost twenty islands of various sizes representing three cultures at which you can anchor your boat every night for months and never stay in the same anchorage twice.

Within three years of Drake's failed attempt, the citizens of Old San Juan once again found themselves under siege, but this time the Earl of Cumberland did conquer San Juan by mounting a landside invasion. The success was short lived, however, because he withdrew from the city six weeks later. An outbreak of dysentery killed so many of his soldiers that he surrendered his prize and to the relief of the *Sanjuanearos* he raised his anchors and simply sailed away. The English invasion caused little real damage, but the occupation hurt Spain's pride, from which Madrid, which was now the capital of Spain, made an important and strategic decision that would affect the island and the people of Puerto Rico up until the present.

A year after the British abandoned San Juan, Spain sent a fresh battalion of four hundred soldiers, forty-six cannon, and a new governor Alonso de Marcado. His marching orders from the Spanish Crown were to wall in the whole city. To offer protection from another land attack, the Spaniards began to build a second fort called *Castillo de San Cristobal*, which was located at the city's east entrance. This public works project was also of the first order taking almost two hundred years to complete, and some men both freeman and slaves spent their entire lives laboring on the walls and fortifications. San Cristobal Fort became El Morro's comrade in the city's defense and when complete in 1771, the dual fortification quickly gained in reputation as the Gibraltar of the West Indies. A massive system of outworks supports the fort, which provided protection in depth, and it is one of the largest defenses ever built in the Americas. Rising to an impressive height of one hundred fifty feet above sea level, *San Cristobal* covers twenty-seven acres of land. As if its size and height were not sufficient to intimidate enemies, its intricate modular design was sure to foil them. It does not seem to be as imposing as El Morro is from the land or from the sea; nevertheless, it is a strategic masterpiece with five independent defensive positions. All five connect by moat and tunnel, and each one is fully self-sufficient should the others fall.

The formidable defenses of *El Morro* and *San Cristobal* again proved their worth in 1797 when they helped a considerably smaller force led by General Don Ramon de Castro repulse General Ralph Abercromby's larger force of reportedly as many as thirteen thousand British troops and German mercenaries, sixty-four warships, and six hundred cannons from besieging the city. After two weeks of fierce fighting, which included prolonged artillery exchanges and even hand-to-hand combat, unable to overcome San Juan's first line of defense, Abercromby gave up. This was to be the largest invasions to Spanish territories in the Americas.

San Cristobal Fortress

If not for these forts, and the bravery of the Spanish garrison and the Puerto Rican militia, then this all out battle royal and most ardent attack with the sole purpose of finally conquering the island would have likely succeeded. If it had, Puerto Rico may very well be known today as Rich Port and San Juan as Saint Johns, with Her Royal Majesty Queen Elizabeth II the recognize head of state. I like the British to the point that I believe they made a terrible mistake in giving up their empire. Some of my ancestors came from England, but the falling of Old San Juan into Abercromby's hands would have been a cultural disaster, because it is impossible for me to imagine the city being anything else then what it is. I

San Cristobal Garrison Barracks

can hardly picture Puerto Ricans taking to the game of cricket, as it is played today throughout the nearby British islands of the West Indies in places like Tortola and Antigua, as well as the U.S. Virgin Islands, and in far off other lands like Zimbabwe, India, and Guyana on the East coast of South America. Neither can I see Puerto Ricans drinking tea rather than their rich mountain grown coffee, nor giving up their world famous rum and coke for gin and tonic.

Crossroads of the Americas
(Encrucijada de las Américas)

Over the centuries, Puerto Rico became the crossroads of the Americas for Spain as well as her enemies, and in time the United States Government came to not only see the military value of this strategic location, but to secretly covet it. Some historians make claim that the Old San Juan fortification was one of the main prizes that the American Military and government had in their crosshairs, which contributed to an eagerness to enter into a state of war with Spain beyond the sinking of the U.S. Maine in Havana, the cause of which was never clear. The Spanish American War *(La Guerra Hispano Americana)* cost the United States three hundred seventy-nine troops in combat and over five thousand to disease, but gained them an island outpost in the Caribbean with a proven military stronghold that they would occupy and put to use for almost one hundred years.

During the British siege of 1797, San Cristobal's powerful artillery successfully defended the eastern approaches to the city. A century later, one of its guns fired the first shot of the Spanish American War in Puerto Rico. On the following day, May 12, 1898, a squadron of a dozen United States war ships launched a daylong bombardment that damaged buildings and terrorized the population, but still had little effect. The North Americans, as did others before them, also came to see the ineffectuality in attempting to take the fortified city by sea or land. With help from a group of Puerto Rican nationalists who wanted Spain completely out more so than they feared the North Americans coming in, which proved to be for the nationalists a deeply regrettable mistake, the United States Army mounted a land invasion.

U.S. troops enter San Juan -1898

With an expeditionary force that would eventually include sixteen-thousand troops, the Yankees *(Yanquis)* landed on the south coast of Puerto Rico at a town named Guanica. Eventually with the rest of the island in the Army's hands, the small Spanish garrison that occupied Old San Juan would have to surrender. Disregarding the fact that in 1897 Puerto Rico had gained self-government from Spain, nevertheless, at the Treaty of Paris that ended the Spanish American war a year later, Spain ceded to the United States the island, which it no longer had title to.

It was the decision made by the Spanish Crown three hundred years earlier to fully fortify the city after the Drake attack that resulted in Puerto Rico being eventually invaded by the United States and placing the Puerto Ricans once again under another colonial ruler.

Although the Americans brought democracy to the island, as with all colonialists, there were grave insensitivities shown. In the case of Puerto Rico, a country that had been in existence for close to four hundred years before the Americans arriving, one of the humiliating acts was changing the spelling to Porto Rico, and imposing English as the language of instruction in the public schools. As the Americans came to under-

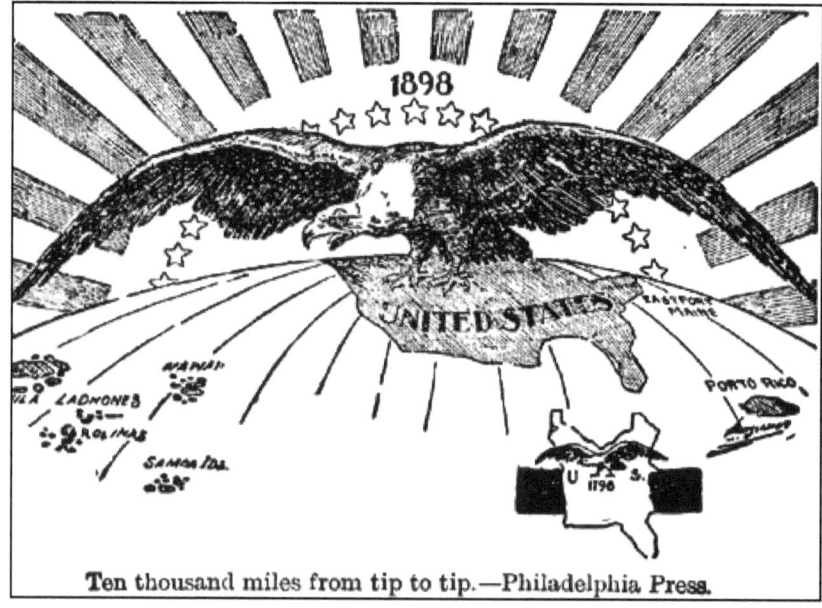
Ten thousand miles from tip to tip.—Philadelphia Press.

stand the depth of the Puerto Rican society, there was a flash of enlightenment with both actions eventually rescinded. In general, and withstanding great social, economic, and political pressure, the people of Puerto Rico with endless displays of patience towards their now somewhat fellow Americans have been successful in maintaining the roots of their culture. Recently the commonwealth party governor of Puerto Rico made the case of maintaining the Puerto Rican culture and language by pointing out to an American interviewer on the Public Broadcasting Television Network that he dreams in Spanish, as do most if not all Puerto Ricans. If asked, the majority of Puerto Ricans would prefer independence, rather than commonwealth or statehood.

PERSPECTIVE

'It has been a SPLENDID LITTLE WAR'

How the United States freed a colony and gained an empire

The pitfalls of imposing authority

Grace of God stills flood of troubles

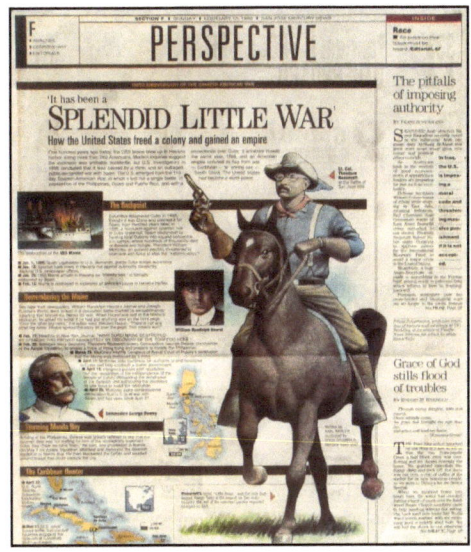

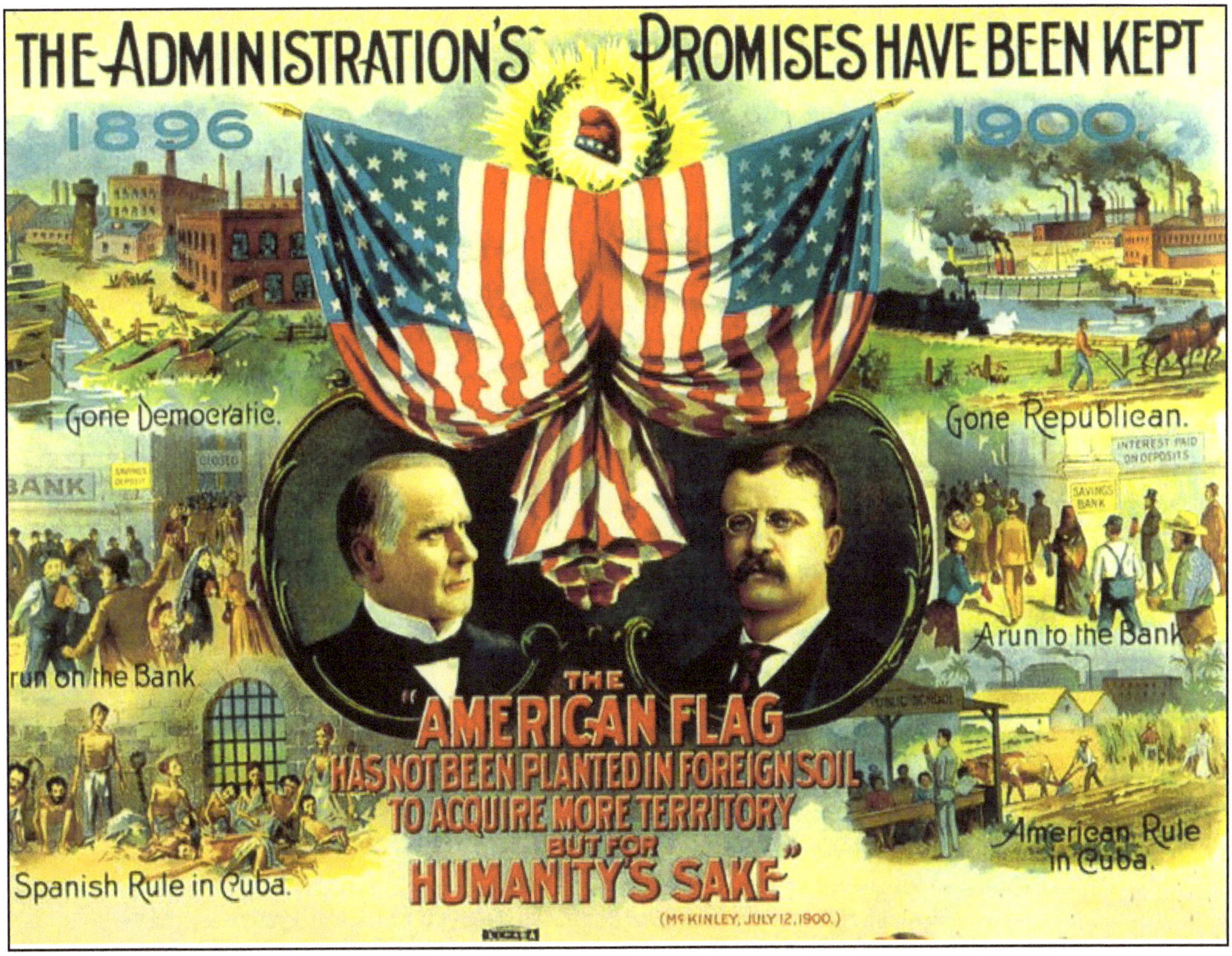

Plaza Colon

Chapter 2

Best of all Worlds
(Mejor de todos los Mundos)

Today, Puerto Rico, and especially Old San Juan, offers the expatriate the best of all worlds, a unique venue and cultural setting within as much of a politically stable environment as can be expected in a Latin American country, were politics and baseball *(politica y béisbol)*, are the two national sports and passionate pastimes. In fairness, Costa Rica still holds the record for political stability of any country in Central and South America, and that Includes Puerto Rico and the Dominican Republic, which, with the exception of Cuba, are the two democratic Spanish speaking island countries in the Caribbean.

Beyond the sun, sea, and palm trees, there are political issues everywhere even in the most idyllic places, like Bali, where in 2002 a car bomb attack at a tourist resort killed two hundred and two people, largely foreign tourists and injured a further two hundred and nine. Almost anywhere, expatriates can be in danger. Puerto Rico is no different, but today, the odds of a political extremist killing an expatriate in Puerto Rico are about the same as it would be in Sweden. Although there is a strong cultural identity among Puerto Ricans, there has never been a widely supported insurgency. Since the beginning of the American occupation, the political contention affecting everyday life that sometimes leads to violence is the unresolved political status question. Statehood, independence, or commonwealth, are the three at odds protagonists, and the issue is as complex as it is the longest running colonial dispute in the world that actually began almost five centuries ago shortly after Juan Ponce de Leon came ashore.

The day I arrived on the island, March 4, 1972, there was an independence demonstration on the campus of the University of Puerto Rico that turned violent. The demonstration was somewhat influenced by the general anti-establishment sentiment and popular opposition to the Vietnam War, which had been part of campus life since at least 1968 throughout the United States. In addition to these issues, there was another and that was the political status question on the island fostered at the university by a very active Puerto Rico Socialist Party, which attracted many students. In addition to its platform of demanding independence for Puerto Rico, it also promoted communism, and its leaders were inti-

mately associated with many of the other socialist causes throughout Latin America and the Caribbean at the time. With the demise of the Soviet Union, the Puerto Rican Socialist Party has also vanished. The Puerto Rican Independence Party (PIP) is still around, but its leaders had never directly promoted socialism, although I suspect many of the followers of the Socialist Party are now active in the only remaining independence party. In my opinion, having been associated with Puerto Rico for 34-years, many who vote for the Commonwealth Party in elections are independence advocates *(Independentistas)* at heart, but that is a topic for another book.

While I was living on the island, however, I never felt in the slightest way of being in danger, nor did I suffer any threats from the many *Independentistas* that I knew and some very well. It was exciting to live in this politically charged environment, which left no doubt that I was residing in Latin America, and over the past three decades nothing much has changed. During my residency, there were a number of violent acts committed by what some would call terrorist, others would label freedom fighters, and still others would describe as patriots, by individuals from the more radical factions of all three sides of the status issue.

Actually, there have been more acts of terrorism in Puerto Rico and on the U.S. mainland committed by Puerto Rican nationalists than by those by Al-Qaeda, although with considerably fewer casualties. Incidents occurred on the island almost from the beginning of the American occupation, but the most daring ones in the continental United States took place during the end of the 1940s and the beginning of the 1950s.

In 1948, Puerto Rican nationalists attempt to assassinate the appointed governor, and in a violent exchange of bullets, all of the five nationalists would die. Two years later, another assassination attempt took place, but this time the target was President Harry S Truman.

During this gunfight, one of the two nationalists and a White House police officer are fatally shot. Five congressional representatives suffer gunshot wounds in 1954 when four nationalists opened fire with pistols in the U.S. House of Representatives. Although in 1999, President Clinton offered clemency to 16 nationalists that were still in federal custody for these and other acts that continued through the 1980s, the status issue still remains and dominates all politics on the island. Freeing these individuals did absolutely nothing to resolve anything, but what it did do was to help his wife's eventual senate campaign in New York, were there is a large Puerto Rican population.

Throughout the late 1970's and mid-1980's the Armed Forces of Puerto Rican National Liberation ("FALN" or in Spanish, Fuerzas Armadas Liberacion Nacional Puertoriquena) and the Popular Boricua Army (Ejercito Popular Boricua), commonly known as the Macheteros, claimed responsibility for numerous bombings and robberies, causing a reign of terror in both the United States and Puerto Rico. The FALN operated in the continental United States, while the Macheteros were active mostly in Puerto Rico.

United States law enforcement first learned of the existence of the FALN on October 26, 1974, the date the group issued a communiqué taking credit for five bombings in New York. . Ultimately, over the next decade, FALN activities resulted in 72 actual bombings, 40 incendiary attacks, 8 attempted bombings and 10 bomb threats, resulting in 5 deaths, 83 injuries, and over $3 million in property damage.

Similar to the FALN, the existence of the Macheteros became publicly known when the group sent a communiqué to the United Press International in which they claimed credit for the death of a Puerto Rican police officer on August 24, 1978. The goals of the Macheteros were complete autonomy and sovereignty for Puerto Rico. In order to achieve their goals, the Macheteros conducted an armed struggle against the United States Government, mainly represented through attacks on military and police, in several cases causing the death of U.S. servicemen. In a January 1981 attack, Macheteros commandos infiltrated a Puerto Rican Air National Guard base and blew up 11 planes, causing approximately $45 million in damages. The capture and conviction of the individual members of the FALN and Macheteros brought an end to the reign of terror in Puerto Rico and the United States. Although a few random assaults may have occurred, mostly in Puerto Rico, the continual assaults on New York, Chicago, and law enforcement and Naval officers in Puerto Rico virtually came to a halt.

Although publicly criticized by many Puerto Ricans, the 1999 Clinton offers of clemency to the sixteen terrorists or nationalist, depending on your point of view, was generally seen as being a act of justice, by most Puerto Ricans in private.

The forts of Old San Juan form an integral part of the contemporary Puerto Rican psyche. So well done was their design as defensive military installations that during the Second World War they were re-commissioned with modern artillery to prevent marauding German u-boats from entering the bay. Even though the cannons no longer serve a military

purpose, and probably will be forever silent, Puerto Ricans see their forts not only in historical terms as a defense of the first order built to protect their beloved city and country, but also as an iconic symbol in defense of their culture. The existence of this walled city for five hundred years and its defenses are so much a part of the Puerto Rican character that it was a terrible pill to swallow when the American military occupied the two forts and the commander of the army new address became *numero uno* Calle San Sebastian, also known as the *Casa Blanca*.

Cobblestones, Silver, and Gold
(Adoquines, Plata y Oro)

Between these two fortifications, and purposely laid out in a Roman military encampment grid, is the beautiful colonial city whose streets are paved with cobblestones (*adoquines*) that were cast from furnace slag. Brought as ballast on Spanish galleons of the treasure fleet, time and moisture have lent them their characteristic cobalt blue color. You can also find the same cobbles in Cartagena, Columbia. In both cities, the Conquistadors generously left the cobbles, and on their return voyages to Spain, they filled the now empty ship holds with silver. Contrary to popular belief, only a small portion of the wealth brought back to Europe from the Americas came from gold. Over the centuries, it totaled a mere five per cent. Spain received the greatest amount during the years of conquest before 1550. Being expensive to mine, most of the gold came from riverbeds near Bogotá, Colombia or from veins of gold found in the silver mines of Mexico and Peru. Puerto Rico likewise produced very little gold with formal production ending in 1570.

The real wealth that built the Spanish Empire *(El Imperio Español)* was in silver, and so much went into circulation that its value, nearly equal to that of gold before the silver boom, dropped to a fifteenth. Nevertheless, when walking around the cobblestone streets of Old San Juan, one begins to grasp just how many ships and how much treasure there may have been.

Narrow cobbled and charming stepped streets, and other quaint pedestrian passages that are hardly more than alleys, all bear false testimony to the grand scale of the dwellings and buildings that face on to them. Interior courtyards in the style of Andulusia in southern Spain, sixteen foot and higher exposed wood beamed ceilings, arches and columns, and grand staircases with hand turned mahogany balustrades; many of the colonial homes of Old San Juan are fit for nobility, and in fact some of these palatial residence were built by Spaniards of royal lineage.

Employing centuries of siege warfare knowledge learned from building the castles of Europe and the bastions of the Ottoman Empire found throughout the Middle East, Old San Juan is one of the world's last great fortifications. Today, nine thousand people call it home and at least twice as many people work in the city. On any given day, there may also be three times that total of visitors. They include both tourists and native Puerto Ricans, since Old San Juan also functions as a commercial shopping center with its boutiques and one-of-a-kind shops, as well as international branded stores. Throughout the United States a new wave of commercial and residential developments are under way that mimics what once was simply downtown. Old San Juan with street level stores and living spaces on upper floors is not only the oldest city under the U.S. flag, but also a fully functioning "downtown" that has been open for business for half a millennium.

Whereas Old San Juan was purposely and for good reason designed to resist attacks, the greatest threat the walled city would face, nevertheless, did not come from outside the battlements. Surprisingly the menace came from inside the city walls. Unforeseen by its planners, an internal peril appeared from an unsuspected direction, and although the English and the Dutch laid siege, each more than once, it was in fact an unanticipated danger from

Best of all Worlds

Casa Blanca

within for which its defensive ramparts were unable to protect it from that almost laid waste to the city. The military engineering of its colossal stone walls and ominous fortifications held off the very determined attempts of the Spanish Crown's enemy's to invade all but once, but the ramparts proved to be inadequate in guarding the walled in city from complacency.

Although many people suffered world wide, the great depression of the 1930s flattened Puerto Rico like an atomic bomb. The 1940s saw some recovery to the island and its economy, but the general population remained broken back poor, children went shoeless, and outside of the few main cities, the country people *(campesinos)* stilled lived in *bohios*, which are huts made from bamboo and thatched with palm fronds. From 1955 to 1980, Puerto Rico accomplished an amazing feat. What it took the United States over one hundred years to realize, the island achieved in one generation.

A predominantly agricultural economy, based on cattle, sugar cane, and coffee, considered one of the best in the world and served at the Vatican, became an industrial economy seemingly overnight. Throughout the island and beginning in the 1960s, many new communities of single-family concrete homes called urbanizations sprung up, and the Puerto Rican society once again found itself under a form of attack, but this time it was a new type of siege called future shock. The Old San Juan defenses that had served the populace so well for so long were unable to offer any protection, and with the twin banners of growth and progress now waving, the city that the bastions enclosed and cannon had defended was being forgotten. Because of the mostly unintended neglect, it was quickly falling into what came close to being a state of irreversible ruin with the municipal government seriously considering plans to demolish buildings in order to make way for parking structures inside this historic city. Hard to imagine, but true.

During its generally unnoticed decline by the majority of the Puerto Rican population, being preoccupied with other social and economic issues, and as an attempt to generate some subsidy form of income, a number of the owners of Old San Juan's buildings subdivided the large residences into smaller apartments. Along its two principal commercial streets, *Calle Forteleza* and *Calle San Francisco*, aluminum, and glass storefronts replaced many beautiful colonial facades. Some business owners, who thought of themselves as being forward-looking, believed that they could stem the tide of the demise of the old city by modernizing the entrance to their stores with display cases behind plate glass windows. By doing this, the merchants' hope was that they could more easily show their products and wares, attract more customers, and increase sales. Moreover, it was often true. Some property owners unable to figure out what to do with their residential buildings simply abandoned them; other buildings suffered vandalism, or turned into what Charles Dickens would describe as being nothing more than hovels occupied by squatters. By the 1960s, Old San Juan was in bad shape, not unlike many cities throughout the United States, and be-

yond that, other cities like London, Paris, and even the prosperous Hong Kong. An urban plague was sweeping across the world, as suburbia was on the ascent, and in its wake, Old San Juan was literally becoming a pile of rubble.

Over the centuries, and because of the Puerto Rico's birthright laws, many of the buildings in Old San Juan went from generation to generation as inheritances. Some of these structures had literally hundreds of owners. Most of whom could not be found nor traced, or simply had no knowledge of having inherited anything. This unintentional and maybe unavoidable legal disarray greatly hindered the sale of scores of buildings, and many heirs saw them as being nothing more than headaches with legal and financial liabilities. Despite all that was wrong, by the end of the 1960s the resurrection of Old San Juan, nevertheless, began.

World Heritage Site
(Sitio de Patrimonio Universal)

While the Puerto Ricans were, and with good reason, building the island's economy and combating a 30 percent unemployment rate, along with some very forward thinking Puerto Ricans, it was also individuals in the expatiate community who early on took up the daunting challenge of rescuing these extraordinary sixteenth and seventeenth century Spanish colonial buildings. Ironically and as a result, it may be that a small band of invading foreigners, for whom the walls and battlements were suppose to keep out, in the end actually gave a hand and helped save the old city. As an architect that lived and practiced in Old San Juan in the early 1970s, I was one of these smitten expats.

La Forteleza and the San Juan Gate

When I first arrived in Puerto Rico, I lived in what was then a small town in a valley thirty miles south of metropolitan San Juan, and although I had heard about Old San Juan, in truth, I really did not know much about it. By accident, I drove into the old city and immediately I became enamored by the architectural beauty. The living history and character of this unique Spanish colonial walled city became even more intriguing, as I learned further about this somewhat forgotten Shangri-la like place. Although life out in the country *(campo)* was also an extraordinary experience for this Manhattanite, I could not resist the draw of Old San Juan and shortly after stumbling upon it, I moved there.

Far from being alone in my deep and growing appreciation, and because of its outstanding universal cultural appeal, in 1983 the United Nations designated Old San Juan as a World Heritage Site for having gained the recognition of being an important legacy for all of humankind. It is a coveted status *(un estado codiciado)* shared with the Pyramids of Egypt, the Taj Mahal of India, and the Great Wall of China. Still today, however, many Puerto Ricans do not fully grasp the full significance, nor the priceless value of what they have entrust. Rather then exploring the heritage of this living theme park with their children, they pack the kids up and head north to Orlando to the make believe world of Disney, Mickey Mouse, and Donald Duck.

Caleta de San Juan

In addition to the whole city being unique, and beyond the incomparable dual fortifications and distinctive colonial buildings, Old San Juan has many special urban elements. One of which is the only tree-lined street in the city, named *Calleta de San Juan*. The name itself offers a hint to this particular street's importance. It begins at the foot of a small hill directly inside the also historical San Juan Gate with its large reinforced wood doors that resemble those of a medieval castle. Opening on to the bay, the construction of this colonial portal began in the late 1700s as one of six sets of heavy wooden doors that were some eight meters high and five meters wide located in the wall that encircles the city. The one at the foot of *Calleta de San Juan* is the last one of the six to survive. For literally centuries, and with strict and punctual formality, the guards closed the doors at sundown to cut off access to the city and protect the citizens from the ever-present danger of invasion.

If you found yourself outside of the walls and on the wrong side of the massive doors after sunset, that is were you spent the night. At times when I walked thru the city gate, during one of my often meanderings and many wanderings in and about the old city, the ambiance that surrounded me made it easy to visualize the bay full of Spanish galleons whose imagined holds were overflowing with treasure en route from South America to Spain. Seeing the ships at anchor in my mind's eye, I could also picture a captain dressed in

the full regalia of a Spanish naval officer disembarking from his ship's longboat at the landing. After sharing salutes with the musket and bayonet toting posted sentinels of the colonial guard, he would stride thru the gate and with swaggering authority make his way to officially report to *La Fortaleza*. It is the governor's offices and mansion, which still serves the same use today and it is within a short walking distance from the city gate.

Best of all Worlds

Cannibals and Barbeques
(Caníbales y Barbeques)

FAMIGLIA INDIANA CARAIBA.

The original purpose for *La Fortaleza*, whose construction began in 1532, was for protection from, not other European empire builders, but the very fierce Carib Indians. They freely traveled throughout the Caribbean not only slaughtering all they came in contact with, but also supposedly devouring those unfortunate souls who were unlucky enough to be captured alive. Sustenance is how the Caribs saw the peaceful Taino Indians who were descendents of the Arawaks that had migrated throughout the Caribbean from South America centuries earlier. During the Age of Discovery, the Carib's cuisine became more extensive. Involuntarily added to the menu were the Spanish, Dutch, French, and English colonists who the Caribs reportedly viewed with great relish. In addition to the words hurricane and hammock having their origins from the Carib language, interestingly and amusingly, so does the word barbeque, as well as the word cannibal. It comes from the Carib word *karibna*, which means person. Amerindians still speak Cariban in northern South America. However, claims of cannibalism in the Caribbean during Spanish colonial times must be seen in light of the fact that Queen Isabella ruled that the only people who are better off under slavery were cannibals; therefore, those who were could be legally taken as slaves. This gave the Spaniards an incentive, as well as an excuse to identify various Amerindian groups as such. One needs to take whole notion of Caribbean cannibalism with a grain of salt.

Known originally as *Palacio de Santa Catalina*, and in addition to being a fort, *La Forteleza*, which is its contemporaneous name, has likewise served as the governor's residence and executive offices from the sixteenth century up to the present. It has the same importance to Puerto Ricans as the White House does for Americans, but its history is more similar to the Kremlin, which in Russian means a fortified town. When Puerto Ricans want to express something about

Palacio de Santa Catalina

someone who has recognized authority, they will often use the name. For example, to relate to you that your wife is calling on the telephone, a Puerto Rican might simply say that *La Forteleza* is on the line.

La Fortaleza

Although this castle-like fort has been the home of one hundred seventy governors and is the official residence of the current one, it was not, however, until 1948 that the first freely elected governor by the people of Puerto Rico, Luis Munoz Marin, moved in. Before the popular vote, either the Spanish kings or American presidents appointed the governor. If the thick colonial masonry walls of *La Forteleza* could talk, they would have just short of five hundred years of political intrigue to report. Because of the ongoing status issue that divides this nation, the plotting is far from being over and the novella that began five centuries ago has a few episodes left. The outcome of the political status of Puerto Rico, statehood, commonwealth, or independence is still a heads or tails toss up.

Beginning from the last San Juan Gate, the *Calleta de San Juan* gently rises up the hill to the front steps of the San Juan Cathedral. Built in the 1520s, as one of San Juan's first structures, the original church had wooden walls and a thatched roof. A hurricane destroyed the church in 1526; the colonists rebuilt it in 1540, the English looted it in 1598, and again the cathedral suffered damage by another hurricane in 1615. The Cathedral as seen today is the result of a major restoration done in 1917. It is an authentic and rare New World example of medieval architecture. The

San Juan Cathedral

placing of the cathedral was a purposeful act of city planning, and a clear example of the Catholic Church's influence. It may very well be here that the naval officer made his first stop on his way to meet the governor in order to thank God for a safe voyage. Before raising anchor and sailing away, it was also customary for the whole crew to make this short pilgrimage up the hill to the Cathedral to offer prayers to God and to the saints. It was with the hope that their incantations would keep them out of harms way as they continue their voyage to Mexico, Columbia, or back home to Spain.

El Convento Hotel

At the top of this unique street and to the left is the entrance to *El Convento*, which was once a seventeenth century convent and today is a delightful hotel. The large and typical colonial open aired courtyard has a lobby bar that serves the world famous made in Puerto Rico Bacardi rum. Its guest rooms have Spanish colonial décor with dark tropical mahogany four posted beds and armoires. *Calleta de San Juan* is not only the most beautiful street in Old San Juan, but also few if any cityscapes measure up to it in any of the state side older colonial cities that I have been to. This includes Dutch settled Greenwich Village, William Penn's colonial Philadelphia, the North End of British Boston, or the French Quarter of New Orleans.

All of these colonial city neighborhoods have unquestionable aesthetic appeal, but from my first hand experience having had the opportunity to live in or visit all of them, Old San Juan has a special feature. As a result of its unique geography and being surrounded by water on three sides, only in this city can you enjoy the colonial ambience without your senses suffering an assault upon turning a corner and having the skyline broken and your sensibilities shattered by the outline of a high-rise building looming in the not so far distance. No matter how initially breath taking or simply beautiful they may originally seem, over time vistas and views often become commonplace. Old San Juan, I suspect because of its size, never got old to me during the years I resided and worked there, and the time that I spent in the city was almost surreal. Other-world-like is the way expat friends expressed to me their comparable feelings from living in other far off and distant lands.

Living Museum
(Museo de Vida)

That which is foreign to us seems to have the greatest impact on our psyche and senses, the outcome of which are deeply embossed memories. When I first arrived in San Juan I sat by the city wall and for hours would stare at the blue green ocean, what a difference than the gray waters of the Hudson or East River that flow past Manhattan. The only thing that has changed in Old San Juan over the last three decades is that within the walls of this five hundred year old city life may be even better *(la vida puede ser aún mejor.)*

Plaza Colon 1896   Plaza Colon 2008

The uniqueness of *San Juan Antigua*, from which it has gained its share of international recognition, is that it is—among other things—very much a living museum. Within it, twenty-five generations have encountered both tumultuous historic moments and long periods of relative tranquility, while residing, working, and experiencing all the joys and sorrow that life has to offer. The Smithsonian Institution in Washington, the Museum of Natural History in New York, and the Lourve of Paris could all fit inside of the walls of Old San Juan with a considerable number of its thirty-million square feet left over. Whereas these formal museums are all institutions that raise their funds with endowments, admissions, and donations, you can enter Old San Juan toll free. Since the city was founded its survival was and still is very much dependent upon the will of its citizens, and today civic pride has replaced the threat of invasion as the primary motivator to keep the city alive, and this form of self-defense is working well.

During the years that I lived in Old San Juan, the waterfront by the bay was not the same as it is now. There were brothels openly operating by the wharfs, which occasionally under political or church pressure the police would halfheartedly raid, and although the following night the bordellos would be back in business, now they are gone. Also missing are the down island schooners that added a Caribbean flavor as a counter point to the more formal Spanish ambience of the old city. They lined the bulkhead at the water's edge with their layback crews patiently sitting by the dock of the bay. Sometimes for as long as a month they would linger while waiting to fill their ship's hold with all types of commercial goods before casting off and beating into the ever blowing easterly trade winds to the Virgin Islands due east and beyond to the other islands of the Lesser Antilles.

Today, the harbor side of Old San Juan has been renovated with new cruise ship piers and terminals, and moored at the other side of the bay are the now diesel powered cargo vessels that have replaced the colorful West Indian sloops. In some ways these changes represent to me sort of a classic expatriate's paradise lost, including smoke filled waterfront bars with seedy characters drinking cheap watered down rum and jumped ship sailors from the four corners of the globe hoping to sneak into the continental United States before being apprehended by immigration officials who would occasionally sweep through. In other ways, with the decks swabbed clean and the grittiness gone, the reclaimed wharfs are safer and available to more then just the deck hands and their simple pleasures.

During the early sixteenth century, San Juan was the point of departure of Spanish expeditions to charter or settle unknown parts of the New World. Rather than traveling back to Spain, San Juan served as home base port. It was here that the fitting out of ships took place and provisions came aboard. An unbroken maritime practice lasting now for over five centuries, for today, twenty-eight vessels call Old San Juan homeport, thereby making it the largest home-based cruise ship port in the world, and each year new ships either originate or call at it. In addition to passenger service, San Juan is the fourth busiest seaport in the Western Hemisphere, and seventeenth in the world based upon container movement.

From the 1940s until very recently, what defined Puerto Rico was the almost mass migration of Puerto Ricans who headed north searching for factory or farm jobs. The migrants had very mixed feelings about leaving the island, as I would come to understand. On a very cold winter's night, a month before I left for Puerto Rico, I was visiting a friend who lived in New York's East Village, which was not a desirable neighborhood back then, but the rents were fittingly inexpensive, if you were willing to share with other tenants a toilet that was down the hall. As two other friends and I were leaving his apartment, a couple with a small child approached us. In broken English and with an accent that my Puerto Rican friend recognized, the male companion asked us for directions. On a tropical balmy evening a few months after, and while overlooking the ocean from another friend's home on the north coast of Puerto Rico in a town of called Aquadilla, the picture of this shivering young couple without proper winter clothes came to mind, along with a question. What would motivate people to leave this for that? Not long after my query found an answer and I came to understand that life in Puerto Rico could be harsh, but those who left, as illustrated in songs like Noel Estrada's poignant ballad, *"In My Old San Juan,"* felt a deep ache of nostalgia. *"One afternoon I departed for a foreign nation that is how destiny would have it. But my heart remained by the sea in my Old San Juan."*

Every Puerto Rican knows this song by heart. When they hear or sing the popular tune tears come to their eyes, because they also know the difficult choices that many friends or family members made when in search for jobs they despondently left the island of enchantment, which is how Puerto Ricans think of their country.

Vital and Dynamic City
(Ciudad Vital y Dinámica)

Although the flame of the love for the old city might have flickered before its resurrection began, gained over the past forty years is a newfound dignity, and today the city continues to evolve while supporting and enriching the lives of the *Sanjuaneuros*, as it always has. In the northwest sector of the city, abutting Plaza San José with its central pediment mounted statue of Juan Ponce de Leon is the new Quincentennial Square *(Plaza del Quinto Centenario,)* opened in October 12, 1992. To me it represents two things. First, it was the cornerstone of Puerto Rico's commemoration of the five hundredth anniversary of Columbus' discovery of the New World, and secondly being the first plaza built in the city in centuries, it is an unmistakable indicator of just how vital and dynamic this city still is.

Plaza del Quinto Centenario

One of its main features is a forty foot high monumental totemic sculpture in black granite and ceramics that symbolizes the earthen and clay roots of the history of all the Americas and is the work of Jaime Suarez, one of Puerto Rico's foremost artists, and a resident of Old San Juan. Other buildings on the adjacent *El Morro* grounds, which had fallen into disuse and disrepair after the United States Army left, went through a dramatic restoration and beautifully readapted to new uses for future of generations to appreciate. Old San Juan is alive and well, as it approaches its own five hundredth birthday. You may not want to miss this *fiesta*.

If any one person were responsible for saving Old San Juan, it would be Dr. Ricardo Alegría. With authority granted to him, as the first director of the "Institute of Puerto Rican Culture," he eventually became an advocate for Old San Juan, and because of his efforts and perseverance, the city became a true "World Treasure."

Dr. Ricardo Alegría.

Beyond receiving numerous awards in Puerto Rico, this renowned archeologist's unique contributions have earned him important recognition, honors, and awards outside of the island. In 1993, the National Endowment for the Humanities gave him the Frankel Prize, which President Clinton presented to him at a White House ceremony. President Francois Mitterand of France awarded him UNESCO's Gold Picasso Prize for his work in helping to preserve Old San Juan as a Historic World Heritage Site. On Dr. Alegría's seventy-fifth birthday in 1996, he received the James Smithson Medal of the Smithsonian Institution honoring his fifty years of extraordinary contributions to Arts and Letter and to World Culture.

In the mid 1970s, our schedules were such that frequently we would share *"Buenas Dias,"* as we passed each other on the sidewalk of Calle San Sebastian, as he made his way to the Institute of Culture offices, which at that time were located at the Casa Blanca, and I was on my way to my design studio. Dr. Alegría was always friendly, but still very formal in his white tropical cotton suit or guayabera, which is a four-pocketed tropical shirt that men wear outside of their pants. It is common wear in all tropical countries from the Caribbean to the Philippines, and throughout other Asian countries such as Thailand, as it is one of my favorite attires.

Best of all Worlds

Calle Cristo Placita

Chapter 3

Passports, Visas, and North Americans
(Pasaportes, Visados, y Norteamericanos)

With all the tangibles and intangibles that Old San Juan has to offer, what makes it even more attractive for especially United States citizens is that there are no cumbersome visa requirements, residency laws, or immigration regulations required in order to migrate to San Juan. Noncitizens must meet the same alien laws as the rest of the country. Although today Puerto Ricans are full citizens with their rights protected under the United States Constitution, Puerto Rico shares, if not a unique, than maybe nebulous is the best way to describe its relationship to the United States. However, do not let the fact that you will find in Puerto Rico things that resemble life stateside, and although many people, but nowhere near everyone, speak English, the Puerto Rican culture is as different and distinct as any Latin American country.

The misperception can fool the unsuspecting, and as a result, many expatriates who for whatever reason come to Puerto Rico suffer classical culture shock when they begin to realize that not all may be what it seems to be. Shortly after arriving, I was fortunate to find myself taken under the wing of another expat who was a long time resident and had made the transition to being completely bicultural. He came to Puerto Rico towards the end of prohibition and surreptitiously opened what today is one of the best-known rum distilleries. When I met him, he had reinvented himself from a bootlegger to a recognized artist. As the founder and primary advocate of Alcoholics Anonymous, he was also a well-known personality throughout the northern Caribbean.

Plaza de Armas 1914

With chameleon like abilities, he was able to make the seamless change from being a North American to, and for all practical matters, a *Puertoriqueno*, seemingly at will. This was at a time in my life when I was still very much a mono-cultural person and had not thought all that much about the nature and influence of culture. When it came to even thinking about identities, as an admittedly young twenty-eight year old back in 1972, I was out for lunch. It even took me a while to grasp what the term "lifestyle" really meant when it became part of the general lexicon during the later 1970s. Nevertheless, what made this person intriguing to me was his acute and conscious awareness of the differences between the Anglo and the Latino cultures, and without being judgmental. He had the second nature ability to intermingle with each equally and at great ease. On the other hand, I have met Puerto Ricans who lived in the continental United States for half of their adult life and Americans who resided on the island for just as many years, and both may have even been bilingual, but neither was bicultural. Disregarding what most people believe, commanding a second language is not a prerequisite for being multi-cultural. A Puerto Rican who accompanied me to the island was fluent in both Spanish and English, but he was a true forget-about-it New Yorker. After arriving, he had a bout of culture shock so bad that within a year he left the island and headed back north to the other island with a substantial Puerto Rican population called Manhattan.

Calle San Francisco 1914

Biculturalism is not the wholesale buying into another culture, nor is it the process of assimilating. I have met expats who by attempting to fully adopt the customs and attitudes of the prevailing culture, even going so far as changing their names, that they became somebody else, to the degree that over time they no longer knew who they were. Overwhelmed by the new culture they suffer a form of the Stockholm syndrome, a loss of personal identity that hostages sometimes experience. What being bicultural means to me, as my friend Abe and mentor pointed out, is the acute

ability to both appreciate and also objectively recognize the differences between your passport and host culture, and just as importantly reject those negative elements of both, and all cultures have them. They may be not only unappealing, but also often harmful. Although few achieve it, for me, becoming bicultural is the epitome of the expatriate journey. It is a state of mind, and after you achieve it, you can easily live anywhere and in the process become multi-cultural, while never losing track of who you are. Choosing to make the trip is more of a necessity for an expatriate than it is really a choice if one desires to be happy, but the trek can be both exciting and great fun, and reaching the destination brings with it many fulfilling rewards. Old San Juan still offers what it always has and whereas the conquistadors found a sheltered bay on their travels back and forth to the New World, so can expatriates find today in this unique walled city a place that also offers a friendly harbor on their voyage of self-discovery.

People leave their passport country for many reasons, and whereas all expatriates are immigrants, in my mind, not all immigrants are seeking an expatriate experience. Some are escaping religious and political oppression; others are looking for a better economic life for themselves and their families. These folks often wind up in an ethnic community in their host country with others from their passport country. All cities of any scale have these ghettos, from San Francisco's Chinatown, to little Havana in Miami, and little Italy in New York. In Sao Paulo, Brazil, you can hear Japanese spoken in the immigrant neighborhoods, like Liberdade. The United Nations estimated 190 million international migrants in 2005, about 3 percent of global population, and no one knows for sure how many illegal immigrants there are all over the world.

Metropolitan San Juan has some ethnic neighborhoods as well, including West Indian, Dominicans, Haitians, Asian, Middle Eastern, and others, but Old San Juan is almost completely homogenized. There is a wide variety of people, including expats from many countries, and although there is one sector of the old city in which almost all of the homes have gone through restoration, the residents in the city make up a general population of mixed diversity. During the years that I lived In Puerto Rico, I encountered very little racial prejudice compared to the United States, which was refreshing, but there are real class distinctions, meaning rich versus poor, much as there is in most other Latin American countries. In addition, among the lower economic groups there are some competition between people of varied national backgrounds, including Latinos such as the Cubans, Dominicans, and Puerto Ricans. Not unlike you may find almost anywhere. Whereas Puerto Ricans view Puerto Rico, more like a country than a state, yet immigration falls under United States federal law. Prior to 911, to travel to any of the island countries in the Caribbean with the exception of Cuba, Americans, Canadians, and many others were only required to have drivers licenses or birth certificates. Today you can not re-enter the United States without a passport after traveling to any of the Caribbean islands with the exception of Puerto Rico and the United States Virgin Islands.

Calle Cristo

Jobs, Businesses, and Generals
(Empleos, Negocios, y Generalissimos)

Work may be the curse of the leisure class, but unless you are independently wealthy and you do not have to seek employment, than compared to other foreign countries, Puerto Rico has its advantages for an expat, especially if you are a United States citizen. What holds many people back from being an expatriate is exactly that, finding an overseas job. As I previously mentioned, but it is worth repeating, United States citizens can work in Puerto Rico without any special work permits or visas. Non-citizens must meet the same requirements as the continental United States.

Puerto Rico and therefore Old San Juan is not for those who are looking to live on a small retirement pension or social security, as it may be possible in other countries. This includes Cuba, Haiti, and the Dominican Republic where the gross domestic product per capita is the highest, but still one third to one fourth of Puerto Rico. Although all three are less expensive, they do not offer anywhere near the same lifestyle that can be had in Puerto Rico. Today, the cost of living in none of the islands in the Caribbean is inexpensive, as it once was even thirty or forty years ago. None of the smaller islands qualifies as being truly Third World Nations, with most being considerably more expensive than Puerto Rico.

When the unemployment rates hits six percent in the U.S. the news media acts as if it is the end of civilization, as we know it. France presently has an unemployment rate of over ten percent, as does other socialist European countries. Third world nations if they did collect information to determine the rate would exceed that amount by at least two, three, or possibly four times. In most of these countries, there is no reason to gather the data since there is no interest on anyone's part to know, or does anyone really believes anyone else is really going to do anything about it. In underdeveloped countries, people have to be more entrepreneurial or self sufficient, which are in truth synonyms, even if what making a living means is collecting firewood or raising vegetables to sell by the side of the road.

Puerto Rico has always been somewhere in between. It is a free enterprise system, with a socialist bent. The economy consists of many small businesses, and an over stuffed centralized government bureaucracy. Because of Operation Bootstrap, which was a tax exemption program that the government initiated during the 1950s there are large international industries also operating on the island. Since its initiation, the type of industries coming to the island changed. As salaries went up the labor-intensive garment industries packed up and left, some relocated to the Dominican Republic. High-tech companies replaced them, and although they required higher skills, they need fewer employees, which contradicted the reasoning for the original exemption program to begin with. The Clinton Administration did the exemption program in, but not until many companies made fortunes and so did many Puerto Ricans. There are jobs available for skilled people in these industries, but the majority of the facilities are located outside of the metropolitan San Juan area, where in the past the unemployment rates were the highest, often reaching 40 percent.

People mistakenly think that tourism is a big contributor, but it only represents less than 10 percent of the island's economy. Because of this misunderstanding, many come to Puerto Rico believing that there is an abundance of hospitality jobs, only to be disappointed.

Finding a job in Puerto Rico is challenging, and although language is an issue, as problems go, it is surmountable unless the extent of your skills is working as a sales clerk, which means having to deal with a predominantly Spanish speaking public. Old San Juan is the exception, since many stores serve the predominantly English speaking tourist trade. Some job advertisements in Puerto Rico state that being bilingual, meaning to be able to both read and write in Spanish and English is a requirement, but what it really means is that knowing English is the real prerequisite. What this translates into is you may very well qualify if you have the essential skills and experience, and you read and write English.

Old San Juan

On line employment sites such as Monster.com, show Puerto Rico as a state, and there are job listings, but not as many as you will see for other states. Puerto Rico is not on the state list for Careerbuilders. The Federal Government also list job openings in Puerto Rico, but some, although not all of them, actually do require people to be able to speak Spanish in addition to English. The island's newspapers have classified sections with job listings and in the Spanish language papers; some of them are in English.

Starting a business in Puerto Rico is relatively easy for anyone as far as government regulations are concerned. There are the typical municipal licenses that you need to apply for, and today zoning regulations are both strict and enforced. Although there is some corruption, it is not anywhere near as bad as you will find in other countries in the Caribbean and in Central America, where to start a business may require making some *generalisimos'* nephew your partner. There is a form of influence peddling in Puerto Rico, and you need to be careful, since most of the time, the so-called influence has very little real sway. Puerto Ricans like to be helpful, but in Spanish, the word *amigo* means friend, but it also means acquaintance, and there is no other word for acquaintance. So when someone tells you that a certain person is his *amigo*, it could very well mean that the person knows him as an acquaintance, but the two individuals do not have a friendship in the English sense of the word, nor does the person have any real influence with the person. It is better to learn patience in trying to get things done, because it is going to take longer to process an application for a business license known as a *patente* than you can ever imagine. In addition, just because someone

has an *amigo* that works in the *patente* office does not mean the process will go any faster. Get use to it, and be prepared for long waits on lines, some of which will probably turn out to be the wrong lines. It would be wise to live in Puerto Rico for a year or more before starting a business, but that would be sound advice no matter where you were moving to, even if it is to a foreign country where you can speak the native language.

Galeria Botello—Calle Cristo

Running a business in Puerto Rico has all of the same challenges as it does any place, but one of the positive aspects of being a business owner are employees. From my experience, Puerto Ricans are very loyal, and work just as hard as any place else, including First World locations. That being said, Puerto Ricans also like to enjoy life, spend time with family, more so than with friends, but when they are at work, they do work. Holidays are important, especially Christmas, which starts actually a week before the twenty fifth of December extends beyond New Years to the sixth of January, which is Three Kings Day and an official holiday. Often people will take their vacations during these weeks, and it is not uncommon for relatives to visit from outside of the island. It is the one time of the year that things really shut down, and many people take time off from work whether they are getting paid or not. It did take me some years to adjust to the idea, but today, and although I have been living outside of Puerto Rico now for some years, I still look forward to taking an extended Christmas holiday.

Third Culture Kids
(Terceros Niños de Cultura)

In my opinion Old San Juan is a difficult place to raise children of school age unless the parents are willing to face the morning rush hour traffic and transport their offspring to one of the many private schools *(escuela privadas)* in metropolitan San Juan. There are children living in Old San Juan, and there was an elementary school, but it has recently been closed and the building turned into a medical clinic. In Puerto Rico the first things parents do when they reach some level of economic means, is to place their children in private schools. The public school system is below stateside standards. Instruction at the primary school level is compulsory between the ages of five and eighteen, and students may attend either public or private schools. There are fifteen hundred and thirty-two public schools and five hundred and sixty-nine private schools on the island. Unlike most schools in the United States, the public school instruction in Puerto Rico is entirely in Spanish, with the exception of one or two metropolitan schools. These schools serve children of returning Puerto Rican families for whom Spanish is spoken at home, but the student has no previous formal instruction in the language. In the Spanish speaking public schools, the curriculum teaches English as a second language and it is a compulsory at all levels. In the early years of the American occupation following the Spanish American War, the opposite was true. English was the language of instruction and schools treated Spanish as a special subject. Considering the fact as previously mentioned that native Puerto Ricans dream in Spanish and think in Spanish, the unfortunate practice fortunately ended in 1915.

San Juan Harbor

As with many Latin American countries, Puerto Rico has a centralized government with a massive inefficient bureaucracy *(burocracia.)* The governor has direct control over almost everything that goes on throughout the island. Without the governor's blessing, very little happens, and even the best of ideas can wither on the vine. There is only one Department of Education for the whole island, and it is a monumental government agency employing some forty-five thousand teachers. With no local school boards, all decisions related to education come from headquarters back in San Juan. With the ratio of private schools to public schools being very high, there is a wide range in the quality of education offered in the private schools, many of which are under religious jurisdiction. Metropolitan San Juan has a number of private schools that are equivalent to a well run stateside private prepatory school. Some offer their curriculum in English and others in Spanish. Along with the wide range of quality there is also a spectrum related to the cost of a private elementary and secondary education. Baldwin and Saint Johns schools are two private nonsectarian English language preparatory schools that are popular with the expatriate community. Wealthier Puerto Rican families also place their children in the English speaking schools, to prepare them for stateside colleges. Tuition ranges from eight thousand dollars per year for lower grades starting with pre-kindergarten, to over eleven thousand dollars per year for the eleventh and twelfth grades. Some of the parochial schools that teach in English are considerably less expensive, but their teaching staff is less qualified, and their school facilities somewhat second rate.

Home schooling as an alternative form of education is legal, but not regulated. There are those in the legislature and the home schooling community who understand there is a balance of interests between state and parents. Although two undesirable and strongly regulating bills did not pass, there is currently a new bill in the House of Representatives that many feel deserving of consideration, with some changes made to it. Others in the Puerto Rican home schooling community are against any form of regulation, no matter how flexible it may be. Those who do favor legislation, which does not equate with regulation, recognize that the lack of public policy in Puerto Rico concerning home schooling has caused much ignorance within the public sphere, as well as within governmental agencies and the judicial system. This lack of awareness has resulted in home schooling parents facing threats of educational neglect and confronting difficulties when having to interact with the government in certain situations.

From my own personal experience, Old San Juan is an ideal expatriate destination for single persons of any age, couples without children, or empty nesters who are seeking to move to a location with a history and a culture that is friendly. As an expat, no matter where you may be interested in going, if you have children you should consider your choices carefully.

Frequently, first generation children of expatriates normally take on most of the significant cultural traits of the host country that they live in, even if they still have names from their parents' passport country. In Puerto Rico, this is no different. Being raised in a cultural enclave, or attending private schools in which the instruction was in their parents' language is not enough to isolate them, and by the time they reach maturity they will be more local in their outlook and values then even their parents may imagine. In some cases, the children have very little contact with their parents' passport country, and simply take on the host country culture, being the only one actually available to them. In other cases, they may maintain some contact with their parents' country of origin, usually because of family ties. Resulting from dual cultural emersion, these children become Third Culture Kids, and they learn to switch back and forth between the home country and host-country as needed, and often develop a truly "bicultural" identity, but not all do.

Instead, they simply identify culturally with where they are. Moreover, whereas their parents may never achieve the status of being a true expatriate, some of the children do, without even knowing that they did. The expatriate grandchildren, who may have even less contact with their grandparent's country of origin, will become almost one hundred percent culturally identified with their birth country. Within the family, there will be very little original passport country influence. Even among American expatriates, who may have experienced the same cultural transformation within their own families, with grandparents immigrating to the United States from Europe or anywhere else, they seldom realize that this process is taking place with their own progeny in their new host country. In three generations, a family can completely transform from being Western European to North American to Latin American, including three language changes. The language conversion of half of my family went from Polish to English to Spanish.

Every Christmas holiday season, a colleague that I knew for twenty years who was originally from New York took his family back "home" to Brooklyn. Eventually he and his wife did move back, but their two adult sons stayed. To them San Juan was home. They never even considered themselves expats. As soon as they got to college age, two children from another expatriate couple that I was friends with left for school back in the states and never returned. Growing up, as a child of an expatriate is often a more difficult life than the parents may realize. At least the parents know the reasons why they are were they are, whereas children often do not. What the kids do know, however, is that while they were growing up, the best time in their lives were the two weeks that they spent every summer visiting with grandma and grandpa back in Ohio were everything worked and everyone spoke English.

Among all foreigners in the host-country, there is a natural kinship. My banker was British who worked for a Canadian bank, and was married to a Puerto Rican. Outside of our business dealings, we shared many insights into our adoptive culture, and we both had somewhat of a different point of view, because of our individual backgrounds. In addition to the Puerto Ricans, I also had an employee from England, a number of Cubans, two Columbians, a Czechoslovakian, and three other expat Americans. Each had come to Puerto Rico under different circumstances and for various reasons, but they all shared similarities. Old San Juan, because of its unique characteristics, attracts people from all over, and the level of diversity is equal to any true First World city. If you take the time and are sociable, you can get to know them. It is a unique opportunity, especially if you come from a mono-cultural place like most Anytown, USA.

Melissa Brayer Hess and Patricia Linderman in their book, *The Expert Expatriate* point out that there are some common characteristics that many expatriates seem to share, disregarding what country they come from. They include; a strong interest in world affairs, a global perspective on the problems facing humanity, open-mindedness and cross-cultural understanding, a love for travel and discovery, a determination to maintain friendships across great distances, and finally adaptability, patience, and an increased tolerance for frustration. They go on to say that, some of these traits may be what lead people to become expatriates in the first place. Finally, they indicate that experiences abroad tend to strengthen all of these tendencies. From my experience people who lack some of these qualities and are especially without tolerance, find themselves on the return flight home sooner than later.

An acquaintance of a friend of mine who lived down island came to save the West Indian souls as a missionary of sorts. She could never overcome what she perceived as the socially accepted loose attitude towards sexuality, which she was unaccustomed to coming from South Carolina. I pointed out to her that if everything on the island were in accordance with her moral standards, what purpose would she be serving by being here. The chat had no effect, since shortly after it she packed up and left.

If for whatever reason you have chosen to be a foreigner in someone else's country, you have no right to expect that the natives be obligated to treat you with any special understanding. While you are playing at being an expatriate, these folks are living their lives with all of the challenges and difficulties that anyone faces, with somewhat fewer options than you may have. It is up to you to figure out how things work, not up to them to make concessions for what they may see in the context of their culture as being only rude behavior, insincerity or simply acts of social inappropriateness. Chances are they know even less about your culture than you know about theirs, and beyond that, they have absolutely no reason or much less a strong motivation to learn. Although, at least one third of all ethnic Puerto Ricans reside outside of Puerto Rico, both in the United States and other countries, for those who have never left the island, even American culture is not something they think very much about or have great interest in assimilating. To them Cousin Pedro, who grew up in Chicago, and comes to the island during Christmas for a visit, is simply an interesting if not odd character.

Many expatriates believe that since they are the aliens, everyone else should be considerate of their circumstance, and if the locals seem not to be then the expatriate feels offended, even when they are the ones that may have broken a social taboo. Every expat or wannabe expat eventually steps outside the limits of propriety or at least makes some guffaw. In Puerto Rico, one can make many. The violation or prohibition and the resulting experience can range from being very amusing to being an infringement that breaks the law, with all the dire consequences that that may bring down. Finding oneself under arrest and incarcerated for any reason in any foreign country is nothing but bad. Going to jail in Puerto Rico may not be as bad as the penal colony in French Guiana that Papillion found himself in, but it will not be as pleasing as a stay at a Four Seasons Hotel either.

An example of a common cultural misunderstanding is that in all Latin American countries including Puerto Rico, and many other cultures throughout the world, there is only one reason why men and women who are not married are alone together. Although to many women the following might sound sexist, in most third world countries women do not invite men into their home with no one else present, unless they are willing. Likewise, women do not accept an invitation to be alone with a man. This includes even the telephone repair or cable TV person. If a man has to enter a women's home or visa versa, then at least the front door should remain conspicuously left open. If not then someone is going to be getting the wrong message, and there is going to be a misunderstanding if not real trouble.

Not only are there cultural problems that an expatriate needs to deal with, but also throughout the world there are issues between expatriates. Not following my own advice, shortly after moving to Old San Juan, I made the uniformed decision to start a business. After hiring an expat carpenter/contractor to do the interior build-out of what was going to be my design studio in Old San Juan, I had an experience that also proved to be classical. Rather than using the funds that I naively advanced to him to purchase materials, he bought a one-way airline ticket off the island, and that was the last anyone saw of him. His behavior seemed rather extreme at the time, but I was also new at being an expatriate. Later on, his action no longer appeared so odd to me. Beyond once also personally contem-

Ponce de Leon Estate

plating my own Dunkirk type of evacuation, I witnessed other expatriates do similar things. This experience was a lesson. Admittedly, as a novice expatriate I felt a sense of ease and camaraderie with this person—something I had not yet fully developed with the locals. He was a fellow expat also in construction, and he sincerely seemed sympathetic to my somewhat disorientation, as a new arrival. In retrospect, I suspect he knew this, saw me as an easy mark, and took the shot. Similar situation and dealings happen regularly between expatriates throughout the world.

Cheerful and Optimistic
(Alegre y Optimista)

A recent study concluded that Puerto Ricans are the happiest people on earth. Attending any function from a birthday party to a wedding reception or any other type of celebration or *fiesta*, one would have to conclude that the finding of the study is all but apparent. Puerto Ricans are inherently cheerful and optimistic, *(alegre y optimista)* which is contradictory to Anglo logic and reason when their collective political and individual economic circumstances are fully considered. The inexplicable social condition of real joyfulness that is reflected in the Puerto Rican character *(caracter de Puertoriqueno)* that some mistakenly equate with frivolity or unreliability, can by itself make an expatriate's life in Old San Juan truly a refreshing and rewarding experience beyond the beautiful colonial architecture, lush tropical climate, and rich cultural heritage.

HORSES BEING LOADED IN SPAIN FOR THE TRIP TO THE NEW WORLD

Life in the old city is similar to living in a Matrioshka nesting doll, but in reverse. There is the inner city world with its charming life inside the walls. Outside is metropolitan San Juan, which is very much a twenty-first century city, and beyond the larger world of Puerto Rico, the isle of enchantment, with all that it has to offer. My other book, *Puerto Rico, Beyond the Shore*, will tell you more about the island. It has beautiful mountain towns that are nestled within lush valleys, plantations where farmers grow the coffee served at the Vatican, a world-famous rainforest with cascading waterfalls and water so pure you can drink it from the ever-flowing streams. Inland are ranches where they breed the celebrated Puerto Rican *pasofino* horses. The name was coined in Puerto Rico, the country of origin of the "fine step," which is the horses' unique and comfortable gait that is a natural result of its genetic heritage. During colonial times horses were Puerto Rico biggest export.

The discovery of extraterrestrial life, if it exists, will probably happen at the *Arecibo* Observatory and radio telescope located on the north coast of Puerto Rico, and about fifty miles west of Old San Juan. Almost everyone has seen it, since a number of flicks including one of the James Bond movies featured it. Cornell University operates the facility under a cooperative agreement with the National Science Foundation.

As related previously, but worth restating, due East of Puerto Rico are the smaller English, Dutch, and French islands of the Lesser Antilles. West of Puerto Rico is the Greater Antilles, including Hispaniola, the shared island of the Dominican Republic and Haiti. Further west and ninety miles south of Key West is the Castro brothers' private island formally known as Cuba. Closer to Old San Juan than Miami is Caracas, Venezuela, which is less than a two hours non-stop flight from San Juan or just a close, is Panama City, Panama, and most of Central America. Rather than flying back to Los Angeles, by traveling the same distance you can go to carnival in Rio de Janeiro, Brazil. If that is to far to travel, you can attend carnival in St. Thomas, which is a fifteen-minute flight from San Juan, or a two-hour ferry ride from Fajardo on the eastern tip of Puerto Rico.

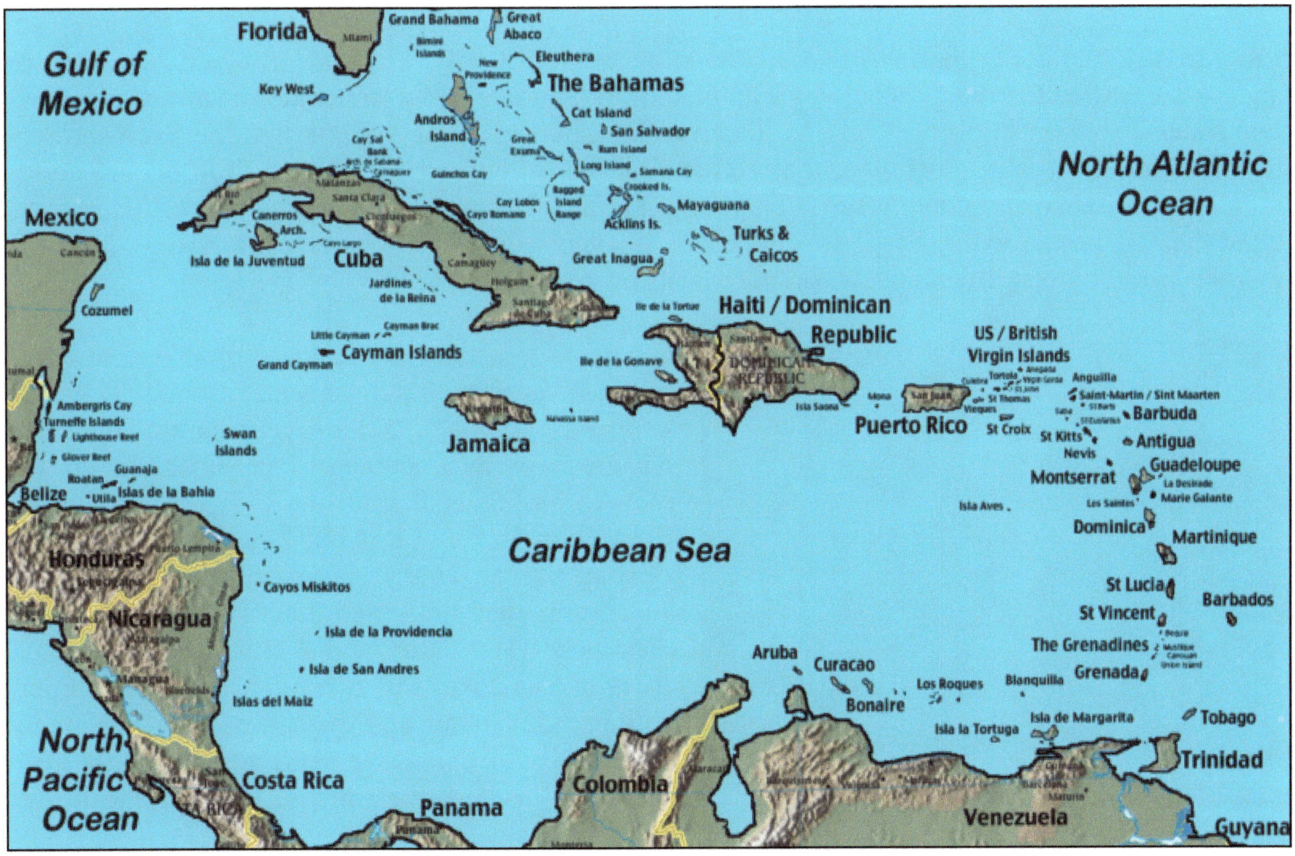

side your air-conditioned soundproof sedan nervously watching and impatiently waiting for the red light to change. It may sound as if I am making a pitch for city living, well I am. Like other cities, Old San Juan offers a newfound freedom from being dependent on a car with everything within walking distance that you may need. Ironically, walking rather than driving, whether it means either strolling to the market or visiting the dentist, can be as liberating as getting your drivers license was when you turned sixteen.

Public Cars and Urban Trains
(Carros Publicos Y Tren Urbano)

Puerto Rico's public transportation system is reasonably good. The Metropolitan Bus Authority (or *AMA*, its Spanish acronym) operates in, as its name says, the metropolitan San Juan area. Bus stop signs read *Parada*, and are magenta, orange, and white. There are also mini-buses called *"carros publicos,"* usually carrying ten to fourteen people. For the past half century, this was the very effective and inexpensive albeit somewhat inefficient mass transportation system. Although they are a good way to get around, and many use the public cars to travel to towns outside of the metropolitan area, be prepared to wait for them to fill up from ten minutes up to a few hours. This method of transportation referred to as a shared taxi is common throughout the world and not only in developing countries.

As with any major city, San Juan's taxis have meters, but to avoid visitor problems, the tourism agency simplified the rate schedule by establishing fixed rates between the airport and major tourism zones. From the airport to Old San Juan is a flat nineteen dollars. Taxis post the fixed and meter rates, and as it is in most other major cities, the fares between pickup and drop off are incremental by distance and waiting time. There are additional charges for luggage as well. However, what there is not an extra charge for multiple passengers, which is a common swindle of out-of-towners, used by taxi drivers the world over from Boston to Bangkok.

Car rental agencies are at the airport and at other locations around San Juan, and throughout the island. All the major rental agencies are in Puerto Rico, as well as a couple of local ones. Expect the rates to be higher than in the U.S., and so will be the amount on hold on your credit card. The *Tren Urbano* (Urban Train) is a new ten-mile rapid transit system that links San Juan's central business districts of Hato Rey and Santurce to residential areas in San Juan, and two other adjacent municipalities, Guaynabo and Bayamon. The new mass transit system that is very efficient, but not very effective, because the route is limited, and it was very expensive to build. Plans to extend the system are in the works, including a branch line into Old San Juan. The expectation is, however, that this expansion is still at least a decade and hundreds of million dollars away.

Driving in Puerto Rico is on the right side of the road, whereas if you go to the nearby United States and British Virgin Islands, be careful, because there the driving is on the left side. In Puerto Rico all road signs are in Spanish, distance markers are in kilometers not miles, and gasoline sales is by the liter. If you are accustomed to paying for your gas by the gallon, when you see the price at the pump do not get excited, because there are 3.7 liters to a gallon. If you multiply the price per liter by four, you will get the approximate

cost per gallon, which is about what you will pay in any east coast American city. A non-resident may operate a motor vehicle in Puerto Rico during the first one hundred twenty days of being on the island, if that person possesses a valid non-expired driver's license issued from anywhere in the United States, or in any foreign country that imposes requirements similar to Puerto Rico to grant a license. For longer stays, any person can obtain a Puerto Rican license by requesting it and paying the corresponding fees, without having to take a test if the person has a current license. You keep your original license. There are over three million vehicles in Puerto Rico, almost one vehicle for each person, and all automobiles are imported, so due to shipping costs and excise taxes the prices are generally higher than they are stateside or in Europe both for new and used cars. During rush hours, the number of vehicles contributes to some monumental traffic jams *(tapons)* especially in and around metropolitan San Juan. Puerto Ricans display endless patience with children, and in general are respectful and polite people. When they are behind the wheel of a car, nonetheless, there is literally a Dr. Jekyll to Mr. Hyde transition. Racecar drivers are more courteous on a NASCAR circuit track. Driving defensively in Puerto Rico is a life or death choice, as it is in Rome and Mexico City.

No matter if you choose to go east or west, or north or south, there is the real promise for exploration, as well as discovery, and all of it is nearby and in a variety of cultural settings not unlike living in Europe. However, Old San Juan was for me so all-inclusive that during the earlier years that I was living there I found little reason and had even less interest in leaving the city, and sometimes I did not venture out for months. The old city can also provide a real sense of remoteness and isolation that some expats seek and even prefer. No matter how emotionally comfortable and pleasant living life within the walls is, the very at hand ability to step out into a completely different world is a bonus that other places just do not have, even those few that may boost a similar ambience as Old San Juan. Cartagena, Columbia is also a Spanish colonial walled city, but considerably smaller than Old San Juan. Greater Cartagena has about half the population of metropolitan San Juan and it is five hundred miles away from the capital of Columbia, Bogota. Although often referred to as the Athens of South America, during the past twenty years it has suffered under the scourge of the cocaine cartels and FARC. It is the Spanish acronym for *Fuerzas Armadas Revolucionarias de Colombia–Ejército del Pueblo*, The Revolutionary Armed Forces of Colombia–People's Army, which are communist revolutionaries and an illegally armed terrorist organization in Columbia.

El Convento Hotel

Cabin fever, sometimes called island fever, is an authentic malady that can change paradise into purgatory, very quick. No matter how long one has entertained the dream of living in the Alaskan wilderness, buying that live-aboard sailboat and sailing off into the sunset, or moving to that tropical island, in reality the experience will only be all that it is cracked-up to be for maybe a year, or possibly two. It does not have to be living in a log cabin, on an island, or a boat that can lead to being stir-crazy; it can happen while being on terra firma in the center of a continent the size of Asia. Any place lacking stimulation caused by physical or intellectual remoteness, monocultural blandness, or even an environ of abject poverty, can trigger a form of cabin fever from which the expat winds up staring into the bottom of a bottle of hooch, depressed. If all you want to do is waste away in Margaretville, buy a Hawaiian shirt, a pair of topsiders, a Jimmy Buffet album, a bottle of tequila, and stay put at home in the burbs. Being a successful expatriate to me means not becoming a drunk, suffering a divorce, or ending up in some backwater jail. It takes work. If you are unwilling to put in the effort, you best make a round trip reservation and keep the return flight ticket handy, because with desperation you will be frantically rummaging thru your suitcase or turning your dresser drawer inside out looking for it sooner than later.

Potpourri of Uses
(Popurrí de Usos).

Before Henry Ford invented the assembly line people walked from here to there. Going out was an event that had greater significance than running to the store, which for many people means driving the SUV a half of mile to Wal-Mart and cruising up and down the aisles while being in the company of mostly strangers. Old San Juan, in addition to its human scale, is a neighborhood that allows for the chance of getting to know the people who you encounter while shopping or passing on the streets, as it is also self-contained. Contrary to modern city planners and their imposed zoning regulations that result in segregated cities and monumental traffic jambs, Old San Juan is a potpourri of uses *(popurrí de usos,)* from stores, offices, and residences, to restaurants, government buildings, and a post office. They all coexist with relative ease.

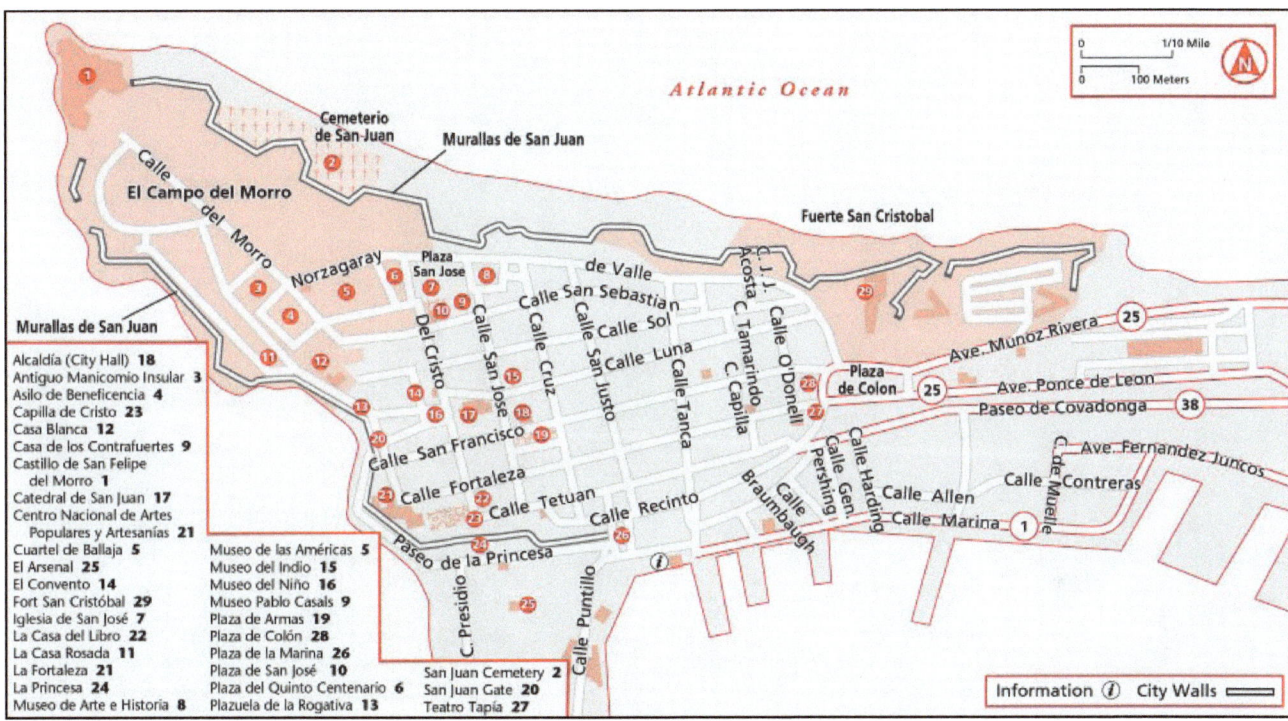

When I lived and worked there, my design studio was on the ground floor of a restored three story small apartment building. The studio with its sixteen foot beamed ceilings wrapped around the interior courtyard, and my sixteenth century Spanish colonial townhouse was only two blocks away. Beyond the pleasant short walk to work, I came to discover that on occasion I enjoyed going back home for lunch rather than always eating out, although within walking distance there were many choices, including a restaurant next door that was run by three expatriate ladies that served great chili. Whereas walking from here to there might seem time consuming, in reality your days will seem longer. Commuting time saved and not having to exert energy driving, one can more readily take pleasure in the sights and sounds of all that is around you more so than you can by sitting in-

A slow night in Old San Juan

Chapter 4

Donkeys, Americans, and Sunburns
(Burros, Gringos, y Quemaduras de Sol)

The map below lays out a walking tour of the city, and shows exactly how much of a pedestrian experience Old San Juan really is. When sauntering around learn to cross to the shady side of the street, because with a sense of amusement any *Sanjuaneuro* will tell you that only donkeys and Americans *(burros and Gringos)* walk in the sun. Because of the southern latitude, every year scores of sunburned tourists painfully find out how dangerous and considerably hotter than even Miami the equatorial rays are.

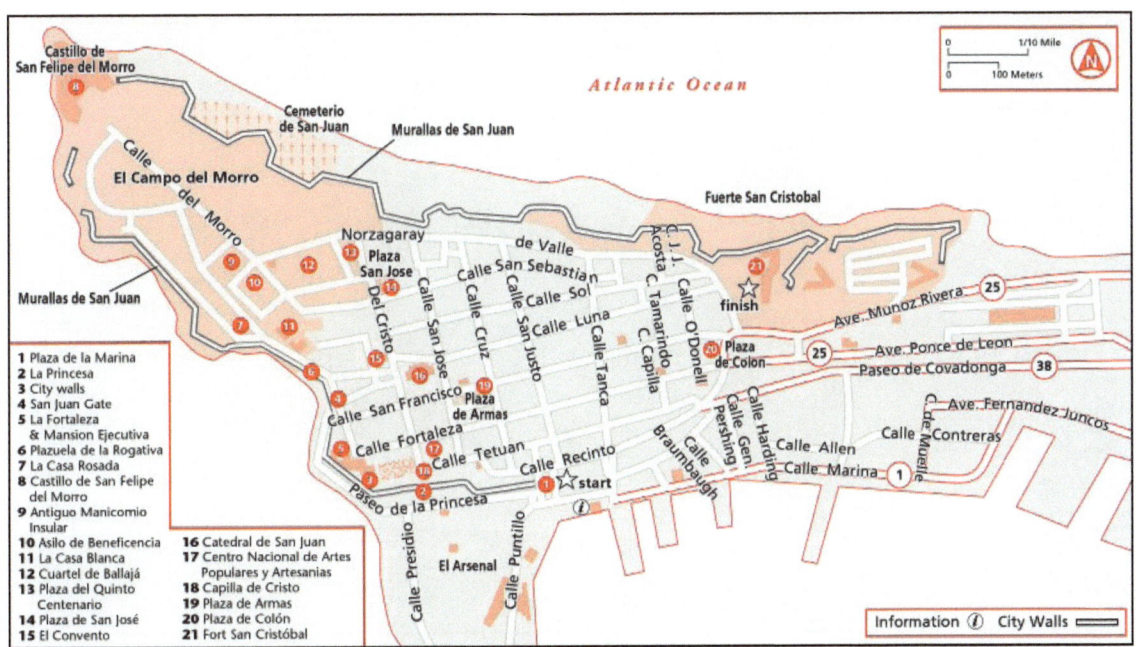

77

If you decide to go to Old San Juan, even just to check it out, you can discover how much fun it is to explore the city by taking a historical cultural narrative and entertaining morning guided walking tour during which you will explore historical buildings and some unique interior courtyards. Contact **Legends of Puerto Rico** on line. Your guide will narrate pirate stories, legends, and historical facts as you visit twelve famous and infamous destinations. You can experience the Puerto Rican culture up close with an alternative non-touristy route so you can begin to feel like a native or resident. Take the evening tour called *Night Tales of Old San Juan*. The program includes love stories and Puerto Rican folklore under the romantic Caribbean stars.

Dining Out—New Latin Cuisine
(De Comedor—Nuevo Latino Arte Culinario)

In addition to the health benefits, that walking offers, if you live in Old San Juan the daily exercise will improve your appetite. The next map identifies some of the wonderful restaurants that you can expect to encounter. Every night for at least a full month, you can dine at a different eatery without eating either the same type of food or dining in the same place twice. Although all of the restaurants are within walking distance, the cuisine widely varies from *criollo*, meaning typical Puerto Rican or local, to classical Spanish fare, and now to New Latin Cuisine *(Nuevo Latino Arte Culinario)*. Today in Old San Juan, as in other cities, a new generation of chefs is creating fabulous original cuisines like that on the menu at the Parrot Club.

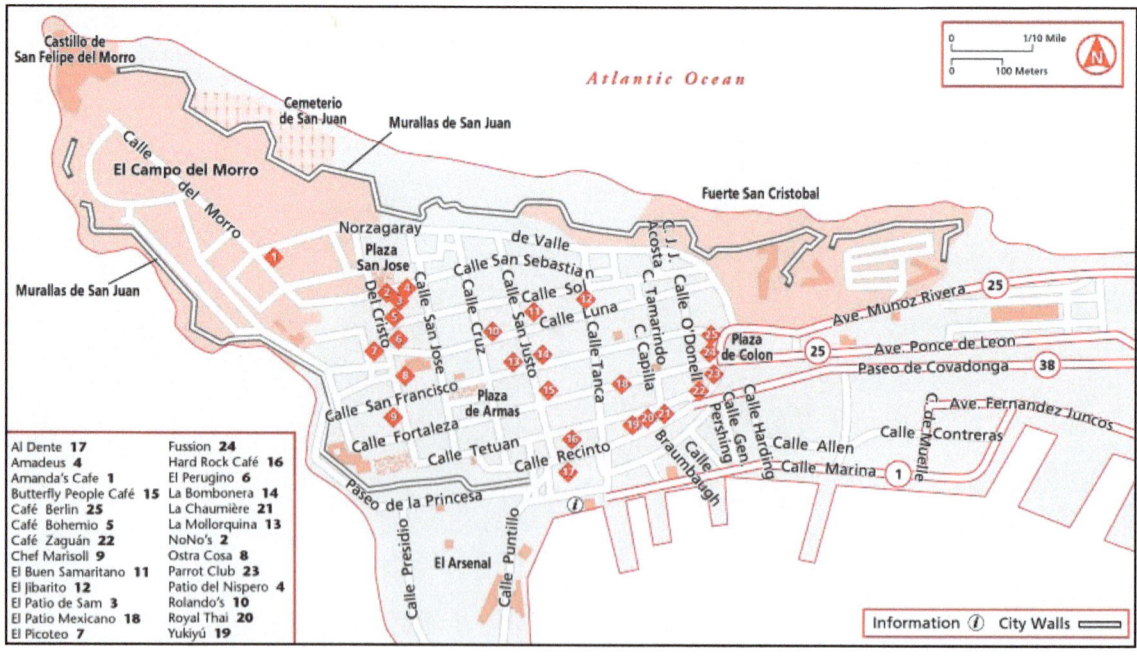

As one of the most sought-after restaurants in what has become the epicenter of Puerto Rican cuisine, it is located in the SoFo district of the old city. That is the sector of the city SOuth of FOrteleza Street. Here a number of very imaginative and unique restaurants are located, including one that serves an Asian Latino Carte du jour. SoFo also has numerous dance clubs, and on holiday nights and weekends, a hip young crowd fills the streets. The Parrot Club bistro and bar serves a new Latin cuisine that blends traditional Puerto Rican cookery with Spanish, Taíno Indian, and African influences. Its setting is a stately colonial building that was most recently a hair-tonic factory. Today you will find a cheerful-looking dining room, where San Juan's mayor and the governor of Puerto Rico are sometimes spotted, and a verdantly landscaped courtyard, where tables for at least two hundred diners are scattered amid potted ferns, palms, and orchids. The rhythms of live Brazilian salsa, or Latino jazz fills the room and spills out onto the cobble streets nightly, as well as during the popular Sunday brunches.

La Chaumiere is reminiscent of a French inn. This intimate two-story restaurant located near the Parrot Club is European in its ambience. Specialties include, of course, French onion soup, and Oysters Rockefeller, rack of lamb, scallop Provencal, and veal Oscar (layered with lobster and asparagus in a béarnaise sauce). This eatery has been under the same management since 1969 and is one of the oldest French restaurants on the island.

On the more traditional side, for breakfast try La Bombonera on Calle San Francisco. With its stain glass storefront and an ambiance reminiscent of a 1950s Madrid pastry shop, it has been a local favorite since 1902. Although I often enjoyed eating there, it was in this restaurant in 1975 that I ate for the first and last time sea turtle soup *(sopa de tortuga.)* After this unique cuisine experience, I made the decision that if I had a taste for seafood I would to stick to the Caribbean lobster, which has a big body twice

the size of its northern cold-water cousin, but with no pincer claws. Not wanting to insult my friend who suggested the choice, and seemed to enjoy his bowl, I forced the mushy meat down, but I could never understand why sea turtles eventually found their way on to the endangered species lists. It certainly could not be because of the way they taste.

For strumming Spanish guitars and a wonderful Castilian dinner, visit *La Mallorquina* on *Calle Forteleza*, a few blocks from the governor's mansion. Most historians believe that this restaurant to have been the first established in Puerto Rico. In 1848, the restaurant's original owners came to the island from Palma del Mallorca in Spain, which is why they named their restaurant *La Mallorquina*. Loosely translated it means *the girl from Mallorca*. If you search, you can also discover the birthplace of the *pina colada*. At the west end of Calle Forteleza near the corner of Calle Cristo, on the front wall of La Bara-china a carved stone plaque makes the asser-tion. For fifty-years, there has been a running dis-pute, however, because the San Juan Caribe Hil-ton Hotel bar makes the same claim to fame. What I suggest is to sample the world-renowned and offi-cial drink of Puerto Rico at both establishments. Decide for yourself who deserves the title, and it may take more than one before you can cast your ballot. There are many different places to eat in Old San Juan, and for every budget, which is exactly what you would expect from a city.

At lunchtime, follow the locals to the Miami luncheonette for a meal of rice and beans with chicken, accompanied by a fresh salad or maybe a side dish of sliced avocado, which in Puerto Rico is always in season. Tipping in Puerto Rico is similar to the states, and in hotels, major restaurants, and nightclubs, service charges are usually included, so check the bill before you unknowingly give a second tip. However, many less expensive restaurants do not add a gratuity. If it is not included, then 15 to 20 percent is customary. In general, service in Puerto Rico is satisfactory and usually friendly, certainly more so than in Paris, but not exemplary, except at the branded hotels where there is training.

Eating In — The Good Life
(La Comida En — La Vida Buena)

If you prefer to eat at home, what you can find in most supermarkets in the states, you can find today in Puerto Rico, although not necessarily in Old San Juan. Puerto Rico has this distinction over other expatriate destinations, especially if you like to cook, or you have holiday recipes that you just have to make. In the 1970s, an entrepreneurial individual began importing fresh produce from outside of the island, and forced the local supermarket chain, Pueblo, to do likewise. Their buying capacity was such that they eventually put him out of business. For many years there was a small Pueblo Supermarket (*Supermercado Pueblo*) in Old San Juan that was adjacent to the San Juan Municipal building, but it was recently closed. There are large supermarkets outside of the old city, which have just about anything you may want, and the closest is no more than five miles away.

On other smaller islands of the Caribbean, including the United States and British Virgin Islands, shopping for the week's groceries often means stopping at three or four different stores and even then coming away with only half of what was on your list. Planning a menu is often futile. It is easier to see what there is in the stores that day and then create your meal around it. Expatriates who live in these places learn to improvise and to make do, or they quickly become frustrated, and many do just that. I recommend giving your recipe book away if you are moving to a remote place. However, if you decide to go to Old San Juan and you just have to have that Christmas pudding, chances are you can find what you need, but you will probably have to leave the old city to do your holiday food shopping. If the reason you chose to be an expat is that you were searching for new experiences, try making new dishes with what is available. Beyond avoiding aggravation, there is an associated health benefit for eating locally grown fruits and vegetables.

An acquaintance that studied at the University of Puerto Rico's School of Public Health, always advised his friends, although they often did not listen, to eat native, no matter where they lived. No, drinking allot of the local Puerto Rican rum is not exactly what he had in mind. According to him, and it seems to make sense, the indigenous foods have the necessary vitamins and enzymes needed to combat local diseases. In Puerto Rico, there is a truckload of choices of local fruits and vegetables. This includes at least half a dozen types of bananas, with one that even tastes like apples. Whether you are in Old San Juan, or wherever you are, for economic reasons alone it is best to go the indigenous route when it comes to food. Those Granny Smith Apples from the orchards of Washington State, which are called for in your great aunt Mildred's apple cobbler recipe, are going to be very expensive when you add shipping costs. Mangos growing on the trees by the side of the roads are not only better for you when you are in the tropics, but they are also free.

Since 1954, Old San Juan celebrates the *Fiesta de San Sebastian* in honor of Saint Sebastian who is the patron saint of young adults and athletes. Originally organized by Father Madrazo, it is a street fair with music, arts, crafts, and food. Every year it attracts hundreds of thousands of people who literally overflow the streets of the old city dancing, singing and celebrating as only the Puerto Ricans know how. In addition to enjoying the festivities, you can prepare the typical Puerto Rican manioc dish, yucca with garlic sauce. The reason I like this simple recipe is that I am a culinary challenged person. First take two pounds of yucca, also known as manioc, and boil it in salted water with ten peeled cloves of garlic. When cooked through, drain all but one inch of water in the pot. Now, in a blender, process eight ounces of corn oil with the boiled garlic cloves and pour over the hot yucca or manioc. Cook another 10 minutes, season with salt and there you have your Puerto Rican garlicky yucca. Enjoy the Puerto Rican good life *(la vida buena.)*

The San Sebastian street party that goes on for four days during the end of January is not, however, an official holiday. The list below names the official holidays that Puerto Rico celebrates. There are a total of nineteen, ten are United States Federal holidays, and the other nine are local to Puerto Rico. These are the official holidays for the commonwealth, and some of the towns throughout the island have there own patron saint day that they observe as well. The nearby Virgin Islanders are no slouches either. They have eighteen public holidays, without counting carnival. Throughout the Caribbean, various islands hold carnival festivals at different times of the year. In the United States Virgin Islands, Carnival events take place on St. Thomas in April/May, St. Croix in December/January and St. John in June/July. Other islands in the Caribbean have other dates, so if you like to party, the West Indies is the place to be.

Puerto Rican Holidays

1 January, New Year's Day—*Año Nuevo*

6 January, Three Kings Day—*Día de los Tres Reyes Magos*

11 January, Eugenio María de Hostos Birthday (1839) Puerto Rican patriot

3rd Monday in January, Martin Luther King Jr. Birth Day

3rd Monday in February, Presidents' Day—*Día de los Presidentes*

22 March, Emancipation Day—*Día de la Abolición de la Esclavitud*

16 April, José de Diego's Birthday, Puerto Rican patriot

Last Monday in May, Memorial Day—*Día de Memoria*

24 June, St John the Baptist—*Santo patron de San Juan*

4 July, U.S. Independence Day—*Día de la Independencia de Estados Unidos*

17 July, Luis Muñoz Rivera's Birthday, first elected governor of Puerto Rico

25 July, Puerto Rico Constitution Day—*Conmemoración del Estado Libre Asociado*

27 July, José Celso Barbosa's Birthday, Puerto Rican patriot

1st Monday in September, Labor Day—*Día del Trabajo*

2nd Monday in October, Columbus Day—*Descubrimiento de América*

11 November, Veterans Day—*Día del Veterano*

19 November, Discovery of Puerto Rico—*Día del Descubrimiento de Puerto Rico*

4th Thursday, in November Thanksgiving—*Día de Acción de Gracias*

25 December, Christmas Day—*Navidad*

Up-to-date Health Care
(Asistencia Médica Actualizada)

Puerto Rico no longer has malaria, but it does have a mosquito transmitting disease called dengue fever *(fiebre de dengue.)* Although it is not as serious as malaria, it can still be fatal for children and the elderly. Balarzia is another tropical disease that one can contract from a parasite carried by a snail found in stagnant fresh water ponds and streams with a slow moving current. Supposedly, the introduction of a predator snail eliminated the carrier, but I cannot imagine why anyone would still chance it and swim or wade in fresh water streams or lakes, with literally two hundred miles of the salt-water beaches available. Dengue fever and balarzia are throughout the Caribbean and Central America according to the Center for Disease Control with malaria still prevalent in the tropical low-lying areas of South America, Equatorial Africa, and most of Southeast Asia, including the Philippines, and parts of Central America. The CDC received reports of one thousand three hundred and twenty-four cases of malaria, with four deaths, that occurred in 2004 in the United States including its territories. All but four cases were in persons who had traveled to a malaria-risk area. Of the four cases in persons who had not traveled, three children had contracted the disease by congenital transmission (from mother to fetus). Malaria still infects between three and five hundred million people every year and causes between one and three million deaths annually, mostly among young children in Sub-Saharan Africa. A friend's father directed the program to eliminate malaria in Puerto Rico, and by the mid 1960s, the island was free from the disease.

The one time I contracted dengue fever I was not living in Old San Juan, but in an apartment on the beach in Isla Verde, which is an area just outside of San Juan. I felt as if a truck ran over me. Fever, exhaustion, and aching joints were the main symptoms, and full recovery took about two weeks. Unlike malaria, dengue is not recurrent without being bit by the little vampire like mosquito again, but it can be fatal especially in small children or people with complications from other illnesses. According to the Center for Disease control, which has offices in Puerto Rico, the disease has cost the island 250 million dollars over that past ten years. For updates on worldwide issues on health, visit the travel section of the CDC website.

If you become ill, or have a condition that requires special attention, San Juan has an abundance of up-to-date medical facilities from major hospitals to every conceivable type of health care practitioner. Many if not virtually all of the doctors speak English, but the nurses may not be fluent. The school of medicine that is part of University of Puerto Rico dates back to 1904. Originally, its focus was on tropical medicine, but in 1948, it became a full medical school. Peoples from all over the Caribbean travel to San Juan for care. If you are a veteran, included in the list of excellent medical facilities is a three hundred fifty-bed Veterans hospital, which recently experienced a major renovation and expansion. The facility provides a full and comprehensive range of patient care, with state-of-the-art technology.

Veteran's Hospital

Considering the volatility and proximity of Latin American the San Juan VA Medical Center has assumed increasing importance for the Department of Defense, because of the departure of the United States from the Panama Canal Zone. In addition, Puerto Rican medical practitioners and health professionals are well prepared to meet any manmade or natural disaster. In Puerto Rico, health care costs are similar to those stateside, because of the technology available and an economy that is not much below the continental United States. Being part of the United States, hospitals and doctors accept Medicare and most health plans, including AARP supplementary coverage.

If health concerns are a factor in restricting your goals of living an expatriate life, then the up to date medical facilities in Puerto Rico can make Old San Juan a very real choice. There are countries in the Caribbean and Central America that are very lacking in health care facilities, and in these places, people still die from relatively simple maladies such as appendicitis.

The Time of Your Life
(El Tiempo De Su Vida)

How often I have heard expats talk about this place or that as being the best-kept secret, but getting there requires traveling half way around the globe. Old San Juan has all of the quality of a far off land, but it is nearby. Direct flights from New York take three and a half hours, from Miami one hour less, and from Los Angeles about eight. With direct flights, also to and from Europe, San Juan International Airport is the hub of the Caribbean and today it has a modern terminal. I have to admit, however, that I miss having to walk down the flight stairs from the plane and strolling across the tarmac to the old tropical terminal. Old San Juan is less than ten miles away from the airport, but an expatriate experience is not only dependent on where one goes.

What it is conditional on is that you go somewhere that challenges your perception of reality or how things are, and Old San Juan will do just that. What is equally important, at least to me, is that in the process of self-discovery, which accompanies the adventure, you have the time of your life *(el tiempo de su vida.)* For many it can begin at the Airport. An extraordinary scene occurs at the American Eagle Airline gates where there is a convergence of local and international traffic, the range of which may not happen anywhere else on the planet. From these gates, travelers board the smaller jets that seat fifty people and turboprop planes that connect San Juan to thirty-five destinations on twenty-five other Caribbean islands of the Greater and Lesser Antilles. The international travelers that connect here are generally coming to vacation, with the expectation of finding relaxation rather than *"un gran revolu,"* which when translated from Spanish to English means a situation of relative chaos and confusion. Naturally, at the airport it reaches a crescendo during the height of the winter tourist season.

A Martinique native may be going to another island less than one hundred miles away, but to get there he must travel to San Juan and sit there for hours to get to where he is going. Frustration levels run very high when you add the "sorting" errors, mechanical problems, lost luggage, and weather-related exigencies when storms are active. Some of the turboprops fly at about ten thousand feet "around" the weather, not over it like the big jets. The result is a bewildering mixture of people, personalities, and cultures. It is a true "callaloo," which is a Caribbean vegetable soup with a concoction of ingredients that is never quite made the same way twice. The

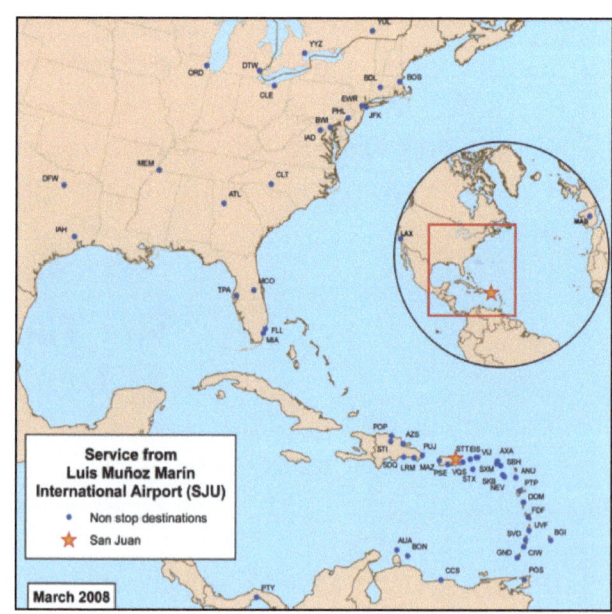

mix at the airport includes interesting local West Indians, who themselves may speak English, French, or Dutch, perhaps with a distinctive island dialect. Add to the blend international travelers from many nations who may speak other languages with a second-language accent, and Spanish-speaking Puerto Ricans airline agents lending another special cultural flavor to what, after all, is their island nation's main airport. Puerto Rico has two other international and seven smaller airports with paved runways that serve other parts of the island, including the out islands of Culebra and Vieques. Because of the climate, which allows for flying all year round, plus the availability of airports, owning a private plane in Puerto Rico is great. Two of my business partners co-owned a four-seat single engine plane, and in addition to using it to visit projects outside of San Juan, we sometimes would fly to Charlotte Amelia in Saint Thomas or Road Town, Tortola for an indulgent lunch.

Law, Order, and the Pearl
(Ley, Orden, y La Perla)

I have met many expatriates who do nothing but complain about their host country, and bad mouth the people whose country they have without asking permission invited them selves to live in. If you cannot handle or appreciate differences, you should probably stay put, although I believe those who are malcontented are so no matter where they happen to be or decide to go. Likewise, if you are maladjusted and that is what is motivating you to get away from where you are, or more likely from yourself, it may be that you are going to find yourself right back from where you began, but probably considerably less well off and maybe even placing yourself in danger. For the discontented person, heading off to some foreign country will only exasperate the condition and the move can be perilous as well.

Like rural areas in other developing nations, in Puerto Rico men walk around out in the country carrying machetes and settle disputes with them. More people own handguns in Puerto Rico than do so legally, and there is still the occasional celebratory shooting of guns into the air, but nowhere near as much as we see in other countries, nor are there any AK47 type weapon at the parties. A typical occasion for festive shooting, normally preceded by considerable drinking, may be when a Puerto Rican boxer wins a title or the Olympic teams wins a medal.

During the past ten years, crime in Puerto Rico is declining. Robberies are down by 64 percent, assaults by 43 percent and rapes by 47 percent. Murders have decreased also, but only by 11 percent, although most are gang killings with drug involvement and take place in the *casarios*. These unmanageable public housing projects are scattered around

San Juan. What was at the time a very socialist oriented government built them during the 1950s and 1960s. As with the many other similar projects built for the so-called proletariat by socialists elsewhere, including the United States, these also became no-man's lands.

Living or visiting in Old San Juan, as with any section of a large city, requires common sense and some vigilance, but within the old city, there is one unsafe neighborhood, and that is The Pearl *(La Perla.)* Actually, it is a separate community outside of the north city walls along the Atlantic Ocean and adjacent to Fort San Cristobal. It was originally the neighborhood where the outcasts of the city would live, as well as some of the poorer military families of the San Juan Spanish garrison. This *"barrio"* was full of wooden huts and notorious individuals. Considered a racy part of town, it is comparable to Hell's Kitchen in New York, years back. The filming of the HBO movie *"Arturo Sandoval, for Love and Country"* took place in *La Perla*, which bears quite a resemblance to many of the *"barrios"* of Havana, and it is similar to the neighborhood where the world famous Cuban trumpeter was born. Although it began as a squatter's enclave, it has grown into a permanent sector of the city with electricity and municipal water service. Whereas numerous city-planning studies concluded that the residents be relocated, during a past election when the outcome of the election was uncertain, the government in power and wanting to remain so actually granted land titles to the residents in an attempt to gain votes. It may have helped, because the party won re-election. Still today, people who do not live there generally do not go there, and this includes the police.

In terms of worldwide crime statistics, keeping in mind that most third world countries do not have the wherewithal to accumulate the data, Puerto Rico ranks twentieth in serious assaults, but still has only about 14 percent of the number that Australia has, which ranks number one per capita. Whereas the Danes, believe it or not, have the most robberies per capita, Puerto Rico ranks sixteenth among developed countries with 72 percent less than Denmark.

Police Air Rescue

Puerto Rico has a 911 emergency telephone number, and the police presence is very visible everywhere, as it is in most American and European cities. Although the police who are on patrol wear bulletproof vests, they do not walk around with assault weapons as they do in Cartagena, Columbia. I drove around Belize not long ago for four days, and during that trip, I traveled north to Corozal, south to Placencia, and west beyond the capital Belmopan thru the Cayo District to San Ignacio close to the Guatemalan border. Except for Belize City where I saw a police officer wearing a British looking pair of white gloves while he was directing traffic, but I do not believe he was carrying a weapon, what I did not see during the whole trip was a single police patrol car. Why I found this unusual is that Belize is somewhat of a Buffalo Bill Cody Wild West show with Guatemalan desperadoes that regularly come across the border, and in the greatest of highwaymen traditions, they stop buses and rob the passengers.

Recognizing that not everything is for everybody, some may find Old San Juan not edgy or challenging enough, preferring the more Third World setting of places like Bluefields on the mosquito coast of Nicaragua or the real end of the world, Port-au-Prince, Haiti. For those looking for a rich experience in a different yet sophisticated culture than almost any other country or city in the Caribbean or Central America, similar to what one encounters in Hong Kong or Buenos Aires, Old San Juan and metropolitan San Juan fills the bill better than even the upstart Panama City.

Americans are so use to negative labels such as "ugly American" that they falsely conclude that all people from other cultures are good. The majority of the populace everywhere is trustworthy and honest, but there are also bad people the world over. In the Third World, countries and it may be a cliché to say, "Where life is cheap," there are, nevertheless, some very bad people.

Navidad in Old San Juan

Chapter 5

Dollars, Quarters, and Pennies
(Pesos, Pesetas y Centavos)

When you in arrive in San Juan by air or sea, you do not have to exchange your dollars into the local currency even though *Puertorriquenos* commonly use the word *peso* for the word dollar and call a quarter a *paseta* and a penny a *centavo*. As a commonwealth of the United States, one *peso* is worth one dollar, and the Puerto Rican *peso* looks just like the American dollar and a *centavo* remarkably resembles a penny. Actually, it is all the same currency, but if you ask for a Coke, few are going to know what you are talking about, because just like other Latin American countries the word *Coca-Cola* is in fact the colloquial version of the brand name. The island, although part of the United States, is in reality a separate country and not just a Hispanic *barrio* as is South Central Los Angeles. Whereas Puerto Ricans have been provisional United States citizens since 1917 and full citizens since 1952, still today, most of the children who are now fourth or fifth generation Americans have difficulty speaking English, as do their parents even though all these families have relatives who live in New York, Chicago, or Miami. In comparison, almost every-

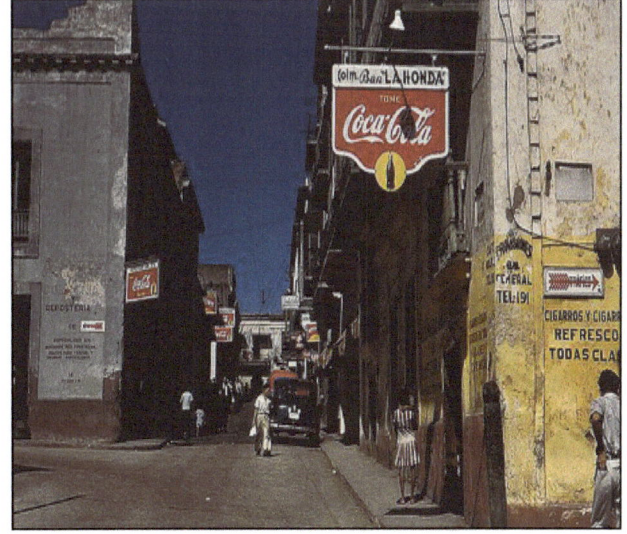

Old San Juan 1941

one in Guam, which became a United States territory, also as the result of the Spanish American War, speaks English relatively fluently.

Most Puerto Ricans consider themselves American, but they are fiercely proud of their island and culture. They do not usually refer to themselves as *"Americanos,"* but *"Puertoriquenos"* or *"Boricuas,"* a term derived from the Taino Indian name for the island *"Boriquen,"* which means: the great land of the valiant and noble lord. To most Puerto Ricans, "my country" means Puerto Rico, and not the United States. This is true even for those *Puertoriquenos* who favor statehood, which is close to 50 percent of the population. Along with this pervasive nationalism, the island has its own Olympic team, and participates independently in the Miss Universe Pageant, which it has won five times since 1970 in a field that has on average 125 contestants. Again in 2006 Miss Puerto Rico, Zuleyka Rivera Mendoza, simply blew away the competition. She too was noticeably not fluent in English, but stunned by her looks I doubt anyone was paying to much attention to what she was saying. Whereas the Ricky Ricardo male stereotype of the Latin lover has been around for decades, the beautiful Puerto Rican women take home the crowns.

Although all Puerto Ricans love their island and it could be said their country, meaning Puerto Rico, many have died defending the United States in every war since 1898, when the United States Army founded "The Porto Rico Infantry Regiment. In 1917 the Regiment was sent to defend the Panama Canal Zone, and after returning to Puerto Rico in 1919 it was renamed "The 65th Infantry. " The Regiment nickname is "The Borinqueneers." It is an all-volunteer regiment of the U.S. Army whose motto is *Honor and Fidelity* and which participated in World War I, World War II, and the Korean War with great distinction.

Master Sergeant Pedro Rodriguez, after serving in a combat role in Europe during World War II, was sent to Korea where in one week he earned two Silver Star medals in addition to a Purple Heart for heroism while under fire. Sgt. Rodriguez retired from the Army with the rank of Master Sergeant and went to work as a mail carrier for the U.S. Postal System in Puerto Rico. He was married to Asuncion Toro with whom he had five children. When he died at the age of 88 in 1999, he was buried with full military honors at Arlington National Cemetery.

Lieutenant Teofilo Marxuach (Retired as a Lieutenant Colonel), a native of Arroyo, Puerto Rico, was responsible for the first bullet shot by the American military during World War I, when he ordered the "Porto Rico Regiment of Infantry" to open fire on the *Odenwald*, a German armed supply ship, when it was trying to force its way out of San Juan's bay. This event occurred on April 6, 1917, the day that the United States declared war on Germany.

Puerto Ricans have participated in every major American military conflict, from the American Revolution when volunteers from Puerto Rico, Cuba , and Mexico fought the British in 1779 under the command of General Bernardo de Galvez, to the present-day conflict in Afghanistan and Iraq. Although somewhat forced into being Americans, they have nevertheless served their second country with honor and fidelity.

Real Estate and Fresh Air Living
(Bienes Inmuebles y Vida de Aire Fresca)

As an architect, I did have an interest, but I never had the opportunity to visit the Bishop's residence in Old San Juan even though I walked past it everyday. It is a very large building on the corner of *Calles Cristo* and *San Sebastian*, cattycornered from *Plaza de San Jose* and Ponce de Leon's statue. Being palatial in scale, it is actually one of the oldest buildings in Old San Juan, which accounts for its rather plain looks, and as a result, it contributes very little aesthetically to the city. In 1511 Pope Julius II appointed Alonso Manso, the Cannon of Salarmanca, bishop of the Puerto Rican diocese; he was the first Catholic bishop to arrive in the new world. My guess is that the bishop's residence (or maybe palace is a more ac- curate term) because of its prime location and size is probably worth ten mil- lion dollars. A past presi- dent of the largest Puerto Rican bank with of- fices in the continental United States and Europe, and one of the top one hundred United States banks, has a residence in Old San Juan, which is reportedly worth four million dollars. I am not certain, however, if this includes all of the tropical colonial mahogany furniture, crystal

chandeliers, and tapestries from Seville, which the home supposedly has. Beyond these two extreme examples and *La Forteleza*, the governor's mansion, there is a wide range of properties in Old San Juan. Most single-family four-bedroom, either a one or a two-storey home, which had a carefully done restoration, would start at one million dollars.

Old San Juan is a unique real estate market because each building, of which there are at least four hundred, is different in almost every way. There is not even one block of cookie cutter look-a-likes. Add to this the location factor, because certain areas of the city may be more favorable, the result is that it is difficult to create comparable prices. To do so, you would have to set up a system similar to the appraisals of diamonds, since no two properties are exactly alike, as well. One rule of thumb may be that, beyond location, the most valuable are those that have original features similar to antiques. This could include the typical grayish-white Puerto Rican marble floors, authentic ironwood (called *ausubo*) beams and the original *tejas* or bricks used during the colonial period for second floor or roof system construction. Scavengers removed beams and bricks from buildings that owners abandoned and sold them in what became a black market of original colonial construction materials during the 1970s and 80s.

What would add more value to a building would be original woodwork, including doors, doorframes, and shutters, even down to the Spanish colonial iron cap and pin hinges, which small foundries located in the Dominican Republic still make. Raising the value of the property higher is hand-carved mahogany balustrades on balconies and interior staircases. Some of which are monumental with hand painted ceramic tiles on the stair risers imported from Spain, the cost of which during colonial times was expensive. These Sevillian tile designs beautifully com-

bine the elaborate floral Spanish style with the geometric symmetry of the Moorish tradition. Although very rare, one can still find at least remnants of frescoes in the homes built originally by the very elite. How these architectural features became lost, it is hard to say, as it is difficult to imagine Carnegie Hall facing the wrecking ball, which it almost did. Before the municipal water supply, all residences and buildings in the old city originally had cisterns with impressive masonry vaulted ceilings. Their constant and cool temperatures make them ideal wine cellars. During restorations, many owners located and excavated them adding spiral staircases for access.

Old San Juan still has un-restored buildings and there is an inventory of buildings and residences that were restored thirty or forty years ago that are due to be renovated with improvements such as new kitchens and bathroom updates. It was common for restoration costs to get out of hand during the 1960s—70s, because of a lack of experience on the part of owners, architects, and contractors. In circumstances when projects overrun their budgets, often the solution is a lessening of the quality of finishes, cabinetry, and kitchen and bathroom fixtures, which always come at the end of a project. Many of these earlier restored buildings solved their budgetary problems exactly this way and they are now ready for makeovers.

Although it is not overly generous, a tax exemption program that waives real estate taxes on both residential and commercial buildings exists for renovations that conform to the Puerto Rico Institute of Culture's guidelines for historic preservation. The government also waives a percentage of income taxes on those renovated buildings, which are income

-producing properties, and conform to the same requirements. As is the case in other historic areas throughout the United States, there are also available federal tax incentives, if you have a federal tax burden. People have bought buildings in Old San Juan to restore and to take advantage of the federal program, but it is not very common since there are no federal income taxes on the island, because there are no federal elections. The local or federal regulations that govern restorations are mostly concerned with keeping the building's exterior true to the colonial architecture of the time of their construction.

There are also rules concerning interior architectural appointments and features such as courtyards and staircases. Many restored private residences have added an extra floor, but there is a set back requirement so that the addition does not change the street elevation of the building. The setback usually becomes an outside deck, and the result is the creation of some very special exterior patio spaces with views to kill for within the city that the original buildings did not have. My home in Old San Juan was initially a one-story building, and because of its location adjacent to the *Casa Blanca*, it was one of the earliest structures built. During the seventeenth century, the building received a second story, and during the building's restoration in the early 1970s a third floor with two bedrooms and a bath followed. At that time, the home had two setback decks on the third floor, one in the front and one in the back plus rear enclosed balconies on both the first and second floors. The street side of the townhouse faced the *El Morro* grounds, and the ground floor of the house was twenty feet above the *Casa Blanca* gardens at the rear. From the second and third floor rear decks, there was a beautiful view of the bay, and in the evening or early morning hours, you would often see cruise ships entering or leaving the harbor.

Because of the homes special location, being the highest elevation in the city, the constant trade wind breezes swept thru the house rendering the decision to air conditioning or not a real toss up. The tradeoff for the fresh air living *(al fresco de la vida)*, which was the choice, was mosquito netting over the beds. During the warmer more humid months, when mosquitoes were more active we would burn mosquito repellent coils in first and second floor living spaces. Normally the incense was required only in the early evening hours during that part of the day when the breezes can actually stop, as the wind's direction changes from blowing in from the ocean to off the land. It is a common meteorological island phenomenon, and the best time of the day to relax and have a cool drink.

As an aside from the main theme of the book, the first night that I slept aboard my sailboat, which I had anchored in a small cove off Palominos Island between Puerto Rico and the island of Culebra, I had a fright. The last thing that I saw thru the opened companionway before falling asleep was the dark profile of the island beyond the stern of the boat. Upon awakening early the next morning, I was startled when I looked thru the same companionway and the island had seemed to disappear. My initial thought was that we had lost the anchor during the night and for the last seven-hours, the boat was drifting off shore out into the Atlantic Ocean. Worse, we were about to hit a reef, since there were many shallows between the island and the coast of Puerto Rico. When I scrambled thru the companionway up on to the deck, I discovered with great relief that the bow of the boat was now facing the island, and we had not gone adrift, but the changing wind had swung the boat around one hundred eighty degrees. I quickly came to understand why the more experienced sailors put out both a bow and stern anchor when spending the night.

Beginning in the 1960s, Puerto Rico played an important role in the creation of the body of laws governing condominium ownership. Although Old San Juan does have some apartments that are income-producing properties, many apartments that are for rent are condominiums so individuals own them, and it is the same for the rest of Puerto Rico. In my estimation, home ownership for Puerto Ricans is a more important goal than it is for North Americans and Europeans. With the exception of Old San Juan, there are few rental apartment buildings in Puerto Rico.

In the old city a rather small studio with a sleeping loft, keeping in mind the sixteen-foot plus ceilings, would begin at six hundred dollars a month, not including utilities. Of the five thousand megawatts of electricity produced in Puerto Rico, only one hundred megawatts are from hydroelectric sources, and although it was attempted and some parts for a nuclear plant were actually bought back in the late 1960s, there are none as of yet. What this means is that the island is dependent on fossil fuels and as such electricity is expensive, and still not fully dependable, although more reliable than it was thirty years ago. In Puerto Rico, many middle class people with private residences have standby generators. From time to time expect to have power outages, and they happen not just when the hurricanes blow thru.

A recent study on Move.com of apartment rents advertised in the United State's twenty-five most populated cities showed that the cost of a two-bedroom two-bath apartment in a restored building in Old San Juan that rents for one thousand dollars per month would be equal to an apartment in Miami, which placed eighth on the list. The apartment would probably not be in South Beach, however, or for that matter on the beach, nor would it have the ambience of Old San Juan and the interior colonial architectural appointments. In New York, which was first on the list and the most expensive, an equivalent apartment rent begins at two and a half times that amount and goes up in proportion to the time spent riding the elevator up to your floor.

Apartments in the Recoleta, Palermo, or Puerto Madero residential sections of Buenos Aires are 40 to 50 percent more expensive than Old San Juan, but like Buenos Aires, and not the states, most of the apartments and homes in Old San Juan come with bidets. One of those civilized plumbing fixtures, whose invention we owe to the French, yet for inexplicable reasons they were not accepted in the states, somewhat like the French themselves. Some believe that the first time Americans saw bidets were in the Paris brothels after World

War II, and this association may be responsible for them not catching on back across the pond. The most historical and beautiful part of Panama City is *Casco Antiguo*, also known as the pearl of Panama. As with San Juan, most apartments in this part of the city are condominiums. Whereas they sell for equivalent prices, rents are 25 percent higher, and the apartments do have some old world character.

An expatriate friend I met in Puerto Rico, who had spent a number of years working for the Peace Corp in Columbia, and then continued living in Bogota afterwards, learned from that experience where to find the inexpensive places to live, and also where the locals ate for considerably less. Old San Juan still offers both, although the less expensive apartments may not be in a restored building with all of the colonial architectural features and charm. It may be in one of the four and five story buildings built over the ruins of a colonial buildings at a time when they were not as valued as they are today. Many of these more or less art deco looking buildings probably have balconies, but chances are there are no courtyards, or high beam ceilings. In the forties and the fifties, under the guise of what some saw as progress, many owners choose to build them.

During the years that Puerto Rico was leaving its agricultural based economy and coming into the twentieth century, a dilemma arose for any owner of a dilapidated Old San Juan building. Why restore a one or two story house, which you may or may not be able to rent or sell because of the limited high-end residential market, when you can build a twenty-unit apartment building whose apartments you could rent? Fair question, and in some ways, it was fortunate that other areas of metropolitan San Juan became popular, because if they had not than very likely many more colonial buildings would have gone the way of the Spanish empire. As with most inner cities, after the Second World War Old San Juan simply became unfashionable like the once exclusive Bedford Stuyvesant section of Brooklyn and its beautiful brownstones with curved glass bay windows.

Blanca Gandhia Realty has been an Old San Juan realtor for at least four decades. This well-known agency has probably sold every building in the city at least once. They are the realtor to go to if you are interested in buying or renting any type of building for any purpose.

Banks, Loans, and "Please Pay Cash"
(Bancos, Pagares, y "Por Favor Paga Cambía")

Banking in Puerto Rico falls under United States banking laws. The Federal Deposit Insurance Company guarantees deposits, and all local banks face the same liquidity and reserve requirements that stateside banks have. There are a number of wealthy local banks, and also operating on the island are stateside, Canadian, and European banks. Most of these offer the full range of services including Federal Housing Administration and Veterans Administration loans, Rural Housing Service loans, conforming conventional loans, nonconforming loans, second mortgage loans, home equity mortgage loans, and other mortgage loans. Services also include commercial real estate loans, construction loans, and consumer loans such as auto loans, personal loans, and credit cards. It is relatively easy to arrange real estate financing in Puerto Rico, compared to other locations in the Caribbean and Central America. One reason is the well-documented registrations of property titles, some going as far back as four centuries, and as a result title insurance is readily available.

In addition to the full spectrum of banking services, between individuals there is another commonly used loan called a *pagare*. This one-on-one financing covers the purchasing of cars, boats, real estate, or anything else of some value. It is a simple loan usually with semiannual payments, and the term is short, seldom exceeding more than a few years. There may or may not be interest charged. All of the terms are negotiable, and what is

The Golden Mile, Hato Rey, Puerto Rico

agreed depends upon how well the parties know each other. In the years that I lived in Puerto Rico, using a *pagare* I bought both a car and real estate.

Puerto Rico has the most dynamic economy of all countries in the Caribbean, including Central America, and although there is a sophisticated banking system, many still live outside the economic mainstream. Forty-eight percent of the population lives below the United States federal poverty line, and the unemployment rate is 12 percent, which is presently more than two times the national U.S. average. Without the means to access the banking system, many rely on the underground or cash economy that includes the *pagare* as an economic facilitator. In the first doctor's office that I visited in Puerto Rico, I was surprised to see a prominently displayed sign that simply said "Please Pay Cash" *("Por Favor Paga Cambía.")*

Lotteries, Taxes, and Amnesties
(Loterías, Impuestos, y Amnistías)

In Puerto Rico, employers withhold social security taxes, but as mentioned previously there is no federal income tax, since residents of Puerto Rico do not vote for the president in federal elections. If a Puerto Rican moves to the states, than as a citizen he or she has the right to vote. The local tax agency, called the *Departmento de Hacienda*, collects a commonwealth income tax. As with almost all Latin American countries, in Puerto Rico the idea of paying taxes, especially income taxes, is not very popular. In 1980, the government held a tax amnesty. The attraction was that there would be no penalties or interest charges if the delinquent taxpayers, or evaders may be a more accurate description, came forward and simply paid his or her back taxes. One hundred thousand people took advantage of the offering, and the majority of those who showed up were from the professions, including doctors, lawyers, and at least one architect. It was so successful, that the government did it a second time.

This inherent attitude towards taxes and the rampant tax evasion that fosters the underground economies prevalent throughout Latin America is why the governments of these countries have historically depended almost exclusively upon lotteries *(Loterías)* in order to raise revenue. Puerto Rico has a lottery that has been around since the Spaniards, and street vendors sell the tickets. Scattered throughout Puerto Rico are also six hundred and fifty off-track betting parlors owned by the government whose revenues also go into the general fund. The wagering is on the thoroughbred horse races held at *El Commandante,* which is a modern race track located about fifteen miles outside of San Juan. In November 2006, Puerto Rico did implement a 5.5 percent sales tax, with the option that municipalities can tack on an additional 1.5 percent. Previously, there was no point of purchase tax, but an import tax. Considering almost everything is imported, almost everything paid a tax. Collection of the tax took place prior to the merchandise leaving the maritime docks or airport. As imports increased, the system became a logistical nightmare. Paying the tax and getting construction materials off of the docks was a difficult as building the building.

Some things are still subject to the import tax, and if you plan to bring a car to Puerto Rico, contact the Office of Excise Tax (787) 721-6237 to determine the amount. You will have to provide information about the car, year, make, model, automatic/standard, number of doors, etc, for the tax to be calculated, and you may want to be sitting down for the answer. There are other requirements that you will need to know if you want to ship a car, including what and what not can be in the car, and how much gas can be in the tank.

Ballaja Military Barracks—Museum of the Americas

Before you decide to ship a car, furniture, or large household items over land and sea remember it may be more economical to sell the them than to ship them. As an example older cars valued at less than one thousand dollars are going to cost more to ship than what they are worth, and in addition they will be taxed. From the United States, shipping cars or household goods can take from seven to fourteen days, beyond the notice time, which may be one to two weeks in advance. Contact a marine cargo company or an authorized trucking company for schedules and rates, and it is best to shop around. If you live in the northeast of the United States, South Florida, or Chicago, you can find Puerto Rican shippers. They usually have the best prices, but maintaining time schedules is another story. Welcome to Latin America, it is where getting down to business means doing it later. Although there is maritime shipping from Puerto Rico to countries throughout the world, in general arrangements are more complicated and schedules are even less dependable.

Temporarily Out of Service
(Temporalmente Ningún Servicio)

Today, most of Puerto Rico has telephone services, and all of the main wireless providers operate on the island, but it was not always this way. When I first arrived to Puerto Rico, the availability of telephones was limited. If you were lucky enough to have a telephone and it stopped working, it could take six months for a repair. Before I moved from the town out in the island into Old San Juan, to make a telephone call would require a trip to the town's main plaza and then an undeterminable wait on

Dollars, Quarters, and Pennies

line to use the "one" public phone that was out in front of the mayor's office. It was always best to have eaten and used the toilet before getting on line. The hope was that whoever it was, that you were calling would be there, and you would not get the all too common message "temporarily out of service" *(temporalmente ningún servicio)*. Actually, the chance of reaching someone outside of Puerto Rico by telephone was better than calling someone on the island. In the 1970s, the Puerto Rican government bought the telephone company. Although I hate to admit it, not believing that the government can do anything right, within ten years it was almost a twentieth century modern communication system. Today the system is back in private hands and a major communications company now owns it. By the 1980s, cable TV showed up. With the arrival of the Internet, the island joined the rest of the world. Old San Juan has everything, telephones, cell phones, cable TV, and there is a selection of Internet service providers.

Before Cable TV, when one of the two local Spanish TV stations broadcast a major movie, it was the Mexican Spanish dubbed version. For the original English soundtrack, you could turn off the sound on your TV and tune in a FM station on your radio. Many Puerto Ricans who spoke English would prefer the original, because the differences in Mexican Spanish versus Puerto Rican Spanish made the translation difficult to understand. It was similar to listening to a movie made in England or Australia for an American English speaker.

WOSO is Puerto Rico's English Language news, information, entertainment, and sports radio station at 1030 on the AM dial. Its programming includes local, national, and international news, weather (although the weather is about the same everyday), and of course being a Latin country political commentary programs featuring local pundits representing the three status issue points of view, plus national broadcasts, such as Dr. Dean Edel and Bruce Williams. There are a select group of music features on WOSO, which include, "JazzQuest" with Hurricane Harry, "The House of Blues," with Elmo Blues, "Super Gold" and "Night Sounds" with Mariano Calderón. Sports programming includes NFL Regular Season Games, with play-by-play radio live coverage.

Cervantes Boutique Hotel

Doors of Old San Juan

Conclusion

Expat Newspapers & Gourmet Coffee
(Periódicos de Expat y Café de Gastrónomo)

As with many places that American or English expats end up, eventually there is going to be an English language newspaper. Founded in 1959 by an expatriate, *The San Juan Star* is a Pulitzer Prize winning paper that offers an early morning edition and home delivery. Over the past forty-five years it grew into a mini media empire with a number of other both English and Spanish publications. It is the only newspaper that I have ever enjoyed reading on a daily basis, and between the end of the 1970s and early 1980s as a contributing writer, I had published numerous articles on architecture, design, and construction management topics in the paper's weekend business section. The *Daily News*, a fictional newspaper appearing in Hunter S. Thomas' bestseller "*The Rum Diary*" is a spin-off of the *Star*. The novel encompasses a tangled love story of jealousy, treachery, and alcoholic lust among the expats who staff the paper. By the time that I began writing for the *Star*, the indulgences and scandalous activities had wound down, if they ever had existed.

Thompson himself traveled from New York to San Juan in 1960 to write for an ill-fated sports newspaper on the island. He had unsuccessfully applied to work at the English-language daily *The San Juan Star* when Pulitzer Prize wining novelist William Kennedy was the editor. While in Puerto Rico, Thompson befriended many of the writers at the *Star*, providing the context for *The Rum Diary's* fictional storyline. Although Thompson wrote the book in the early 1960s, its publication was not until 1998. A movie based upon the book and starring Johnny Depp, Benecio del Toro, and Nick Nolte will be in theatres in 2012.

You can no longer read *The Star*, which after five decades is no longer published. You can read the *Puerto Rico Daily Sun* either sitting on your balcony with a view of *El Morro*, or in your private interior courtyard surrounded by lush tropical plants while enjoying a cup of *Café Rico*. Although it is considered a gourmet coffee brand worldwide, being an island grown coffee, everyone drinks it in this world-renowned Spanish colonial walled city, which is still vibrant and alive after five hundred years. *San Juan Antigua*, built as a defense of the first order, is waiting for you to explore and discover what you may treasure most. This Guardian of the Spanish Main could help satisfy your emotions and fulfill your personal expectations at whatever being an expatriate means to you, as it did for me. In this unique city, founded by Juan Ponce de Leon the most famous of all conquistadors, there are rich experiences still at hand that will leave you with vivid and fond memories of living in a far off, but not to distant land.

Old San Juan Street Signs

Spanish Colonial Interior

About the Author

Seagulls and Sunsets
(Gaviotas y Ocasos)

March in New York is still the winter, and it was on a frigid sleeting early March day when James Tate left his Greenwich Village apartment for JFK airport where he was to catch a TWA flight that would arrive in San Juan around noon. As the straining 747 was about to lift off the runway, the outer engine on the starboard wing exploded sending the plane literally bouncing down the runway. After the passenger's anxieties had subsided an eerie silence filled the cabin for what seemed like an eternity until the pilot calmly made an announcement that apparently the engine had ingested a seagull, and that the plane would return to the terminal. Six hours later the author boarded another flight, but what he did not realize was that upon his arrival in San Juan the delay would result in the first of many treasured experiences that he would have over the next twenty-five years as an expatriate.

In 1972, to disembark from the plane in San Juan you had to walk down the portable flight stairs and cross the tarmac to the terminal building. The author recalls, as if it was yesterday, upon stepping through the fuselage door and onto the flight stair landing, the surprising sensation he felt. He was not prepared for the unexpected blast of hot humid air that hit him in the face, considering the cold weather he had just left. At the same moment, he further relates, the salty smell of the ocean became apparent, and after a brief pause at the top of the stairs his eyes focused on an unforgettable vista. He remembers how he was gazing at the El Yunque rain forest mountain range, which was glowing in a golden green. The setting tropical sun was illuminating the western slopes of the mountains with such intensity that the outline of individual palm trees were clearly discernible in the not to far distance. The triple assault on his senses at that intense moment left him in no doubt that he was about to enter a different world. The morning's incident, which the author admits had filled him with a degree of apprehension of maybe being a bad omen or an ominous sign of things to come, was actually responsible for the evening's astonishing coupled event. "That night I had difficulty sleeping, James recollects, I was anxious to get on with this new life in this exotic place."

After an international career as an architect, contractor, and real estate developer, when reminiscing of the not so long ago past, it is the images and experiences as an expatriate that still fills his mind. Many remembrances are associated with Old San Juan, where he lived and practiced architecture after moving to Puerto Rico now thirty-six years ago. One of the author's goals in writing this book is to share the imagery and insights gained from an expatriate life and in the process encourage others to live their own adventure. And if not in Old San Juan, then another far off, and maybe even a more distant land.

Palacio Verde

Los Puertorriqueños

Bonus Chapter

Who are the Puerto Ricans?
(¿Quiénes son los puertorriqueños?)

Zuleyka Rivera
Miss Universe 2006

A recent study concluded that Puerto Ricans may be the happiest people on earth. You only have to attend a birthday party, wedding, or any Puerto Rican gathering to see that this could in fact be true. At the end of this section we will discover that there may be a scientific reason for this cultural reality, and Christopher Columbus himself was the first to report it.

Old San Juan is a microcosm of Puerto Rican culture, which is somewhat complex and very diverse. Culture is a series of visual manifestations and interactions with the environment that make a region and/or a group of people different from the rest of the world. Puerto Rico, without a doubt, has several unique characteristics that distinguish the Puerto Rican culture from any other. One of the most important influences can be traced back from long before the Conquistadors anchored their galleons in San Juan Bay and came ashore.

The people of Puerto Rico represent a cultural and racial mix. During the early 18-century, the Spaniards took Taino Indian women as brides. These were not common-law marriages, but legal nuptials, fully recognized and encouraged by the Catholic Church. Contrary to some notions, the Indian population was not eradicated, but transformed, as were the Spaniards, the early arrivals from Spain *(España)*. Today 70% of Puerto Ricans have Indian genes. As labor was needed to maintain crops and build roads African slaves were imported, followed by Chinese immigrants. Latter, Italian, French, Irish, German, Corsican, British, Lebanese, Jews, Iranian, and Palestinian immigrant groups (Among others) came to the island. American expatriates began arriving after 1898, and the influx of North Americans never ended. Long after Spain had lost control of Puerto Rico, Spaniards continued immigrating to the island. The most significant new immigrant population arrived in the 1960s, when thousands of Cubans fled from Fidel Castro's Communist state, including a second wave of Chinese from Cuba. The latest arrivals to Puerto Rico have come from the economically depressed Dominican Republic. This historic intermingling of such diversity has resulted in a contemporary Puerto Rico practically devoid of racism. Over the decades that I resided in Puerto Rico, I never heard a racial slur from a Puerto Rican.

Not everyone in Puerto Rico has a Spanish sounding last name, such as Lopez or Garcia. Today, many Puerto Ricans have surnames that clearly reflect the multiplicity of immigrant groups. They include; Wong, O'Neil, McClintock, Chardon, Stubbe, Bini, Feldstein, and Tate to name only a few. The average Puerto Rican turns out to be, in fact, not at all typical.

Oscar de la Renta
Fashion Designer

Sonia Sotomayor
U.S. Supreme Court Judge

Geraldo Rivera
Attorney and Journalist

Richard Carmona
Admiral and Surgeon General

Many Puerto Ricans call themselves Boricuas, which is an Amerindian term. Before the first European contact, the inhabitants of Puerto Rico were part of the Arawak group of Amerindians. They called the island, Borikén (alt. Borinquén) and themselves "Boricuas". They were named by Christopher Columbus in 1493 as the Taíno. Columbus made an acute observation of the character of the Taíno Indians, which still applies to the Puerto Ricans today, and there may be a scientific reason why!

A recent study of Mitochondrial DNA (mtDNA) from 800 individuals found that patrilineal input, as indicated by the Y chromosome, showed over 70% of Puerto Ricans could trace their ancestry to male European ancestors, 20% could trace it to male African ancestors, and less than 10% could trace it to male Native American ancestors.

As for maternal DNA, 61.1% of those sampled were found as having Amerindian maternal mtDNA. This means that if you could trace back in time from daughter to mother, you would eventually reach women who lived in Puerto Rico in Pre-Columbian time. The rest divides between 26.4% with female African ancestors and 12.5% with female European ancestors.

Both of these findings are consistent with the popular belief from historical record that male European immigrants took for themselves wives from among the native Indian and, later, black slave populations.

Dr. Juan Martinez Cruzado, a geneticist from the University of Puerto Rico Mayaguez who participated in the design of the mtDNA study, said accounts of life on Puerto Rico in the 17th and 18th centuries describe many aspects that are totally derived from Taino modus Vivendi, not just the ham-

Benicio del Toro
Academy Award Actor

Antonia Novello
U.S. Surgeon General

mocks but the way they fished, their methods of farming, etc... It is clear that the influence of Taino culture was very strong up to about 200 years ago. If we could conduct this same DNA study on the Puerto Ricans from those times, the figure would show that 80 percent of the people had Indian heritage," according to Dr. Martinez.

Columbus and his crew, landing on an island in the Bahamas on October 12, 1492 were the first Europeans to encounter the Taíno people. Columbus wrote: "They traded with us and gave us everything they had, with good will… They took great delight in pleasing us… They are very gentle and without knowledge of what is evil; nor do they murder or steal." Columbus further reported to Queen Isabella I and King Ferdinand II that in the entire world there can be no better people. "They love their neighbors as themselves, and they have the sweetest talk in the world, and are gentle and always laughing." Although many groups of people have come to Puerto Rico over the last 500 years, remarkably these same qualities are still very observable and widespread throughout this now mixed population. It could be that along with hereditary physical traits, behavior may be as well.

As a counterpoint, in the United States, up until the past sixty-years intermarriage between immigrant groups was less usual and only within the past generation has there been any significant intermarriage between racial groups. In actuality interracial marriage was not only thought of as a taboo, but in some states it was illegal. Not so in Puerto Rico. The lack of racism plus Taino DNA both may contribute to making the "average" Puerto Rican, who she or he is, one of the happiest people on earth.

It is very well likely that DNA does play a role in at least one area in which Puerto Ricans have excelled. Since the formation of the Miss Universe competition in 1952, and with an average of thirty-countries competing, Puerto Rican women have won the crown five times. Only the United States with seven wins and Venezuela with six wins have done better. An important fact that needs to be considered is that the Puerto Rican population is one-tenth of a percent of that of the United States, and one-percent of Venezuela. It could be said that when considering

Jose Feliciano
Musician, Composer, and Singer

Beyond Genetics
(Más Allá de la Genética)

Puerto Ricans are well represented in all fields of endeavors, from beauty queens to scientists, and from entertainers to sport figures. Among famous Puerto Ricans there are also US Army generals, US Navy admirals. Sonia Sotomayor is of Puerto Rican heritage and is today a Justice of the United States Supreme Court. There are other Puerto Ricans who are globally known, such as: Oscar de la Renta, *a leading fashion designer, and* two-time winner of the American Fashion Critic's Award. José Feliciano, known to some as the "greatest living guitarist", is also a singer and virtuoso guitarist, known for many international hits. Others in the entertainment business include; Ricky Martin, a worldwide famous pop singer, and Jennifer Lopez, who is an American Golden Globe-nominated actress, Grammy Award-nominated singer, record producer, dancer, fashion designer and television producer. She is the richest person of Latin American

Jennifer Lopez
Entertainer

descent in Hollywood according to *Forbes*, and the most influential Hispanic entertainer in the U.S. according to *Español's* list of "100 Most Influential Hispanics". She is one of the most prominent Latin American performers in the world, and a recent American Idol judge.

1815 Royal Decree of Graces
(Real Decreto de las Gracias)

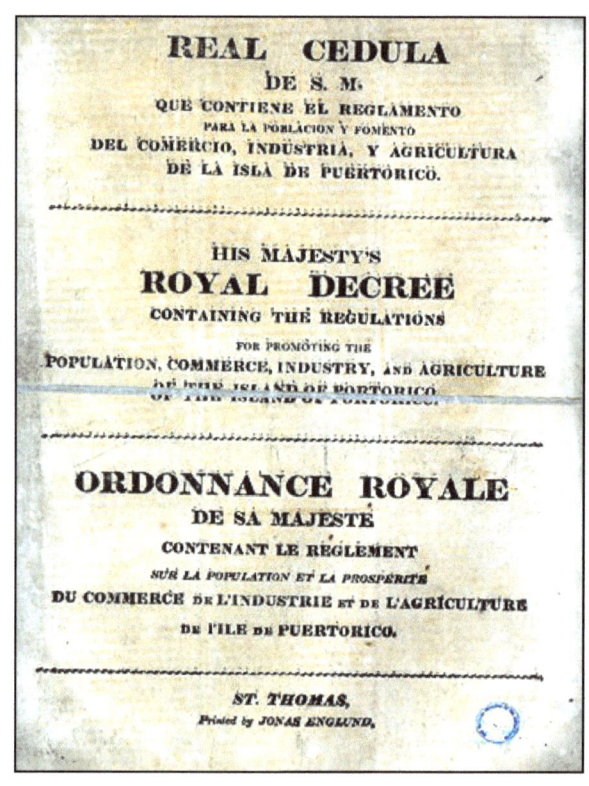

At the beginning of the 19th century, the Spanish colonies in South America, under the leadership of Simón Bolívar and José de San Martín, fought against Spanish rule; and in Mexico, under José María Morelos. By 1825, the Spanish Empire had lost all of its territories in the Americas with the exception of Cuba and Puerto Rico. These two possessions, however, had been demanding more autonomy and had pro-independence movements since the start of the movements in 1808. Realizing that it was in danger of losing its two remaining Caribbean territories, the Spanish Crown revived the Royal Decree of Graces of 1815. This time the decree was printed in three languages — Spanish, English and French — intending to attract Europeans of non-Spanish origin, with the hope that the independence movements would lose their popularity and strength with the arrival of new settlers. Free land was offered to those who wanted to populate the islands on the condition that they swear their loyalty to the Spanish Crown and allegiance to the Roman Catholic Church.

About 450,000 European migrants settled in Puerto Rico. The settlers who took advantage of the opportunities presented by the Royal Decree soon adopted the language and customs of their new homelands and intermarried with the local members of the community. Many became prominent business and political leaders. The Royal Decree was in effect until 1898 when Spain finally lost her last two possessions in the New World to the United States as an outcome of the Spanish-American War. The original Spanish Royal decree of Graces of 1815 is currently kept in the General Archives of Puerto Rico in the Institute of Puerto Rican Culture in San Juan, Puerto Rico.

Notable Puerto Ricans
(Notables los Puertorriqueños)

Since this book is both about the history of Old San Juan and the present, there is one specific group of accomplished Puerto Ricans who have a legacy that goes back to the fifteenth-century. They hold not only a current place in history, but because of their endeavors, as scientists and astronauts, they are standing at the threshold of the future.

In 1581, Juan Ponce de León II, the grandson of the Conquistador Juan Ponce de Leon, studied an eclipse and its effects on the island and was able to establish the exact geographical coordinates of San Juan with his astrological observations. He may have been the first Puerto Rican scientist.

Juan Ponce de Leon II

Joseph M. Acaba
Astronaut

Puerto Rican scientists involved in the United States Space Program, also known as the National Aeronautics and Space Administration (NASA) have made marked contributions. According to an article written by Margarita Santori Lopez for the official newspaper of the University of Puerto Rico's Mayagüez Campus, "Prensa RUM", of the 114 Hispanics working at NASA Goddard Space Flight Center in Maryland alone, 70 were Puerto Ricans or of Puerto Rican descent.

On May 6, 2004, Joseph M. Acaba became the first person of Puerto Rican heritage to be named as a NASA astronaut candidate, when he was selected as a member of NASA Astronaut Training Group 19. He completed his training on February 10, 2006 and was assigned to STS-119, which flew from March 15 to March 28, 2009 to deliver the final set of solar arrays to the International Space Station.

A list of all of the notable Puerto Ricans would fill a book. For those who have an interest in learning more about these accomplished people you can visit:
http://en.wikipedia.org/wiki/List_of_notable_Puerto_Ricans.